IGN TOURING ANC

PROVENCE

"BORIE" AND LAVENDER, APT

This guidebook forms part of a new series of regional touring and leisure guides to France and is produced in association with the French national mapping agency, the Institut Géographique National.

Feature articles trace the history, culture and architecture of each region and detail the prime sports and leisure pursuits available to holidaymakers. These are complemented by a gazetteer section which provides information on resorts and places of interest.

Through the exclusive use of IGN's superb topographical mapping, the motoring tours and walks outlined in each guide aim to help you discover new aspects of France. Above all, though, it is our hope that these guides open the door to your own discoveries.

**Published by McCarta Limited in association with
the INSTITUT GÉOGRAPHIQUE NATIONAL**

We particularly thank Patrick Goyet and Pauline Hallam of the
French Government Tourist Office in London.

First published in 1992 by
McCarta Limited
15 Highbury Place
London N5 1QP

in association with

Institut Géographique National
136 bis, rue de Grenelle
75700 Paris

Publishing Director Henderson McCartney
IGN Coordinator Nathalie Marthe
Series Editor Catharine Hutton
Project Coordinators Folly Marland, Ruth Keshishian
Editors Christian Senan, Lesley Young, Daphne Terry
Contributors Catherine Bray, Helen McPhail, Serge Gas
Series Art Director Prue Bucknall
Designer Colin Lewis
Line maps and illustrations Colin Lewis
Translation Bookdeals, Simon Knight
Research Alex Broner, Pierre Janin
Photo Research Christine Altur
Typeset by Colin Lewis & Associates, Weybridge, Surrey
Printed and Bound by Grafedit, SpA, Bergamo, Italy.

British Library Cataloguing in Publication Data
Provence - (IGN touring and leisure guides)
1. France
I. Institut Géographique National
II. Series 914.4904838

ISBN 1-85365-252 - 0

Photographic Credits
AUBERGE DE CASSAGNE 120, C.D.T. DES ALPES DE HAUTE-PROVENCE
Hughes BEESAU 25, 30, 87, 89, 91, 104, C.D.T. BOUCHES DU RHONE/
SCOPE 34, JEANNEAU Christian FEVRIER 26, EXPLORER 15, 76, 82 (top),
Thierry BORREDON 80, Georges CARDE 17, 33, 73, 85 (bottom), 92, Yves
CAVAILLE 22 (bottom), R. CLAQUIN 107(bottom), B & J Dupont 96, Philippart
de FOY 21 (bottom), 97, GOUDOUNEIX 1, F. JALAIN 11, 20 (top & bottom),
44, 57, 59(top), 70, 72, 74, 75, 78, 107 (top), 110, KALICANIN 113, Louis-Yves
LOIRAT 8, 45, 63, 106, 108, 109, **MAS DE LA
BRUNE** 121, **MAS d'AIGRET, LA** 119, NADEAU 59 (bottom), Philippe ROY
62, 82 (bottom), 111, Philippe ROYER 32, 95, Erik SAMPERS 51, Pierre
TETREL 21 (top), N. THIBAUT 4, 12, 27, 94, 100, Guy THOUVENIN 18, 23
(top), 118, Le TOQUIN 6, 9, 42, Alfred WOLF 7, 16, 22 (top), 28, 55, 85
(top), 98, Henri VEILLER 5, 48 (top & bottom), 65, **S.M.N.L.R.** Le BLANC
29, **VTT, RANDO 04** 35.

CONTENTS

AN INTRODUCTION TO PROVENCE

What does Provence evoke in the mind of a man living the hurried life style of the late 20th century if not the slower-paced life associated with sunshine and holidays?

The Mediterranean folk have a word for it, "farniente": the art of doing nothing, lazing about in the sun or shade, playing boules beneath the plane trees, taking a siesta, waiting for the evening breeze in an open-air café, putting off till tomorrow what you could do today. Perhaps you will learn the art here in Provence.

But Provence also means a distinct culture, a unique history, a beautiful natural environment, leisure pursuits and entertainments (doing nothing while cultivating the appearance of activity). This guide is to help you discover the silence of its Romanesque abbeys, the bustle of its festivals, the parched garrigue, the welcome breezes of the coast. It will save you time: time you can spend in true Provençal style.

NATURE AND THE LANDSCAPE

THE SPECTACULAR AND THE SEDUCTIVE

Bordered on three sides by the River Rhône, the Alps and the Mediterranean sea, Provence is a blend of widely varying landscapes. Human habitation, concentrated in general on the rich plains beside the Rhône and along the coast, has brought fundamental changes to features and countryside, but vast areas of inland and pre-Alpine Provence still retain their natural heritage of great beauty virtually unaltered. Many nature parks and reserves have been established to protect this wealth; particularly along the coast, more coveted and thus more threatened.

In the north-east of Provence, on both sides of the upper Durance valley (from Manosque to Sisteron), still covered with olive and fruit trees, lie the sharp outlines of the great mountain massifs; half of this area lies at altitudes between 500 and 1500m. To the north are the rearing outlines of the Lure and Mont Ventoux, its forest mantle sheltering the sheep-cropped mountain pastures. In the heart of Provence crops appear on the plateaux of Vaucluse, St-Albion and Valensole, with alternating heathland and lavender fields. Lower down, the southern slopes of the Lubéron hills bear the first vines to carry the official appellation 'Provence'. These are regions of scattered and very ancient dwellings, with dozens of little villages perched high, sprawling up the hillsides or nestling into them, dotted across vast expanses of unspoilt natural terrain.

Le Ventoux, a protected site, its white limestone top capped with snow in winter, offers a variety of plant life, meridional on its southern slopes where cedars take over from heathland and alpine on the north with oaks, cedars and pine trees giving way to firs and larch with arctic species such as the little Greenland poppies or the Spitzbergen saxifrage. Early summer brings a colourful spread of flowers blazing across the spreading green pastures, while autumn expires in flashes of flame-coloured forests. The north-westerly winds, with the famous Mistral reaching gust speeds of 290km/hr, fully justify Mont Ventoux's name and ensure a permanent freshness in the air on its northern side through the hottest of summer days.

THE PETIT RHONE

The plateaux of Vaucluse and Valensole make up the middle heights, with gorges or *cluses* and narrow valleys marking out different sections. Vaucluse and Albion consist of porous limestone rock through which the rain water filters down to mysterious underground courses, emerging eventually at the spring of Fontaine-de-Vaucluse. The dry soil nurtures the lavender which is produced commercially, growing amongst pale stretches of heathland, while on the richer soil of Valensole the lavender fields are interspersed with wheat. The cornfields are limited to the south by the River Verdon, another protected site, its torrential green waters tightly constrained within spectacular gorges.

The Lubéron mountain and its necklace of hills provide shelter for an exceptional range of fauna and flora, their fragile equilibrium the object of the specialised attentions of the Parc natural régional du Lubéron, established in 1977. Its damper northern slopes overlook forests of young oaks, the favoured site for truffles (plateau of Les Claparèdes), while vineyards cling to the sunny southern flanks. The Mistral blends together the scents of the gorse-covered heath and the *herbes de Provence* which grow abundantly on these rocky heathlands. A region where game, including wild boar, still abounds, the Lubéron is also the hunting territory of various increasingly rare birds such as Bonelli's eagle, the short-toed eagle and the eagle-owl.

The Ste-Baume and Maures massifs in south-east Provence are noted particularly for their vast spreading forests. The immense cliff-face on the north side of the Ste-Baume (protected site) shelters the plateau of Plan-d'Aups, covered by a magnificent forest of trees several hundred years old : this is a sacred site where no felling has ever been permitted and a wide variety of tree species exist here - durmast oak, dogwood, maple, ash, beech, yew, buckthorn, elm, poplar, Norway pine, sycamore, lime and aspen. The variety of shrubs and flowers is equally wide, combining to make this site an exceptional wildlife haven.

The forests of the vast Massif des Maures (60 km by 30 km) bear the scars of ancient fires, areas invaded by the *maquis* of arbutus, heather and broom. A few sweet chestnut trees can be found here and there in the cooler areas, cultivated for their nuts, but it is the oak tree which reigns supreme: durmast, evergreen or cork oaks. The mountain massif is clearly defined among the other Provençal mountains of limestone base by the crystalline rock structure which links it to the Esterel.

These mountain ranges give the Mediterranean coast, between Marseille and Hyères, a distinctive character, with the famous *Route des Crêtes* and the many *calanques*, sea inlets of sand and rocks beneath impressive cliffs.

Off the Hyères coastline lie the islands of Porquerolles and Port-Cros, both covered with vegetation which, although less varied than that of the mainland, is no less striking. The interior hillsides are covered with cinerarias and euphorbias, myrtle and olive trees, arbutus, Aleppo pines and evergreen oaks. Protected by its status as the Parc

FLAMINGOS - FOS

National de Port-Cros, the seductive natural setting of these islands combines the charms of the great beaches bordered with pines on the northern coasts with the wilderness of sharp cliffs on the southern shores, home to multitudes of sea birds and migrating species.

Marine parks have been established to keep this coast accessible, in the bay of La Ciotat and on the Côte Bleue (Carry, Ensuès, le Rove, Sausset), in addition to the *conservatoires du littoral* (coastal protection sites) at Giens, Carqueiranne, le Pradet, Bandol, Cassis, l'Estaque and in the Camargue. The plains of La Crau and the Camargue make up this unique site of south-west Provence which stretches from Arles on the Rhône delta.

On the left bank of the River Rhône lies the plain of La Crau. Irrigation has brought cultivation to its northern section - olives, vines, almond trees - and its meadows produce the Crau hay, unique in France in possessing *appellation contrôlée* status (similar to that granted to wines) and used to feed the famous merino sheep of Arles. The meagre stony grasslands of the dry southern Crau provide 'free-range' pasture for flocks of sheep. Sheep-rearing, like bull-breeding, is traditional in the Arles region; the shepherd used to be a 'man of the north' from the Durance valley, known as Gavot, who would follow his sheep everywhere in their semi-nomadic wanderings. Traces of this traditional pastoral life can occasionally be seen, a few low stone shepherd huts built in the last century still surviving. Bird life in the Crau, as in the Camargue, includes many and varied species, some extremely rare or near to extinction. Under the title of the Parc naturel régional de Camargue, the Camargue plain has been a protected area since 1970. Its 85,000 hectares include the reserves of the Vaccarès and the two Imperial lakes, all three intended to preserve the fragile balance of an eco-system which is unique in France, the result of the combined influences of the Rhône, the sea and the winds.

The high Camargue spreads out to the north of the delta, a cultivated area of drained salt-marshes now irrigated with fresh water from the Rhône to grow various crops, animal fodder, fruit and vegetables and vines. Rice is cultivated in *clos*, enclosures covering some several thousands of hectares which are flooded from April to September.

The intermediate zone round the pools and lagoons is given over to horses and bulls, kept in herds or *manades* and supervised by their *gardians*. For a long time the gardians' houses in the Camargue - an area without building stone - were made of reeds and plant stems, while the wealthy owners brought in stone from Fontvieille or Beaucaire to build their *mas*. The region's other natural resources are the fish in the pools (eel, shrimp and mullet), and the game which is hunted in the marshes.

The Imperial and Vaccarès lake reserves support an almost equally abundant range of flora and fauna: asphodels, thistles, juniper, iris, daisies, narcissi, tamarisk; beavers, otters and coypu; plus nearly 400 bird species, a third of which are migratory: egrets, marsh-harriers, duck, herons, flamingos, coot, black kites, moorhens, teal, terns and sheldrake.

Salt marshes lie at the two furthest ends of the delta, their vast surfaces divided into geometric evaporation pans; the 'crop' derived from this sea harvest can be seen close at hand every September, in the form of the great piles of salt known as *camelles.*

The rich plain of the Comtat Venaissin lies on the east bank of the Rhône once it has passed the Alpilles hills with their spreads of olive trees. Fruit-growing and market-gardening occupy the valleys round Avignon, Carpentras, Cavaillon, Châteaurenard and Orange. Often protected from the Mistral by screens of reeds, poplars or cypress trees, orchards of cherries, apples, pears, apricots, almonds and olives, fields or little plots of melon, tomatoes, courgettes, asparagus, garlic and onions form a chequer-board across the landscape. Vines spread over the hillsides, growing grapes for the table or for the impressive Côtes du Rhône appellation wines such as Châteauneuf-du-Pape and Gigondas.

HISTORY AND CULTURE

OCCUPYING INFLUENCES

Those who live in other parts of France or elsewhere in Europe traditionally see Provence as an idealized land, a concentrated essence, a holiday setting in a sun-tanned haze of good living. The reality is more complex, however, for the region's identity is as varied as its geography and its culture and way of life, typically Mediterranean, the result of a very wide range of influences and 'invasions'.

Modern Provence lies at the heart of the southeast, fringed to the south by the Mediterranean Sea, to the east by the Alps and to the west by the rich plains which border the River Rhône. Down the ages its frontiers have seldom remained settled as the land passed under the controlling sway of Celtic, Greek, Latin, Germanic, Saracen, Italian, Spanish and Angevin control.

UNDERGROUND ROMANESQUE CHAPEL, ST-PIERRE

From pre-history to the Christian era
Home of the Ligurian tribe during the Iron Age, Provence was gradually invaded by Celtic races from the north who together created the combined Celto-Ligurian civilization. Traces of their characteristic dwellings can still be seen in the form of the 'oppida' or fortified hill-top villages (such as Entremont, near Aix-en-Provence) and the shrines erected to the cult of dead warriors, as at Roquepertuse. The carved ornamentation visible here already showing Greek influence.

Trading links with Greece began several hundred years before the Phoceens settled in the Gulf of Lacydon where, around 600 BC, they founded the city of Massalia, later Marseille. This Hellenistic enclave in a Celto-Ligurian country which later became a Roman province was to remain a focal point of individuality and separatism. The city played a determinant role in 'Mediterranean' history when in the 2nd century BC it sought help from Rome, its ally, against a Celto-Ligurian coalition. The conflict

was settled by the founding in 123 BC of Aquae-Sextiae, Aix-en-Provence, at the foot of the conquered and ruined Celto-Ligurian capital of Entremont.

Roman towns and colonies expanded throughout the south of conquered Gaul, now a 'provincia romana': at Apt, Avignon, Carpentras, Glanum, Riez, Vaison and above all Arles, which inherited imperial favour after Julius Caesar's victory in 49 BC over Marseille (which supported Pompey). The 'pax romana' meant prosperity for the whole of Provence and under Roman guidelines trade expanded, crop culture improved (wheat, olives, vines) and roads and aqueducts were built. The big cities enjoyed the luxury and refinements of Latin culture, and grand monuments were built.

A slight decline began in Provence, however, in the 3rd century AD, particularly as the expanding aristocracy encroached on democratic principles. In 325 AD the fading Roman Empire became, under the Emperor Constantine, a 'Christian Empire'. During the period of chaos surrounding the fall of the Roman Empire in 476 AD the region was occupied first by the Visigoths, who captured Arles in 471, then by the Ostrogoths in 508, and was finally annexed by the Frankish kingdom in 535. Throughout these troubled times it was the bishops who maintained relative order and protected the cultural heritage.

The High Middle Ages
From the 6th century to the early 12th century Provence passed through several hands: shared out between the descendants of Clovis, allied to the Saracens during the revolt against the Frankish king Charles Martel (736-739), integrated into Charlemagne's kingdom (late 8th century), pillaged by the Saracens who returned in the 9th century, shared out again between the descendants of Charlemagne, absorbed into the kingdom of Provence and Burgundy (855) and attached to the Holy Romano-Germanic Empire (1032). Princes, kings and emperors all claimed the province as their own, but were often content with a theoretical act of ownership while local power remained in the hands of the Counts of Provence.

Provence under the Catalan Counts
In the middle of the 12th century Provence included a marquisate on the west bank of the Rhône (Argence and Beaucaire) and in the north (Orange, Vaison and Carpentras), under the government of the Counts of Toulouse. Corresponding to the greater part of modern Provence, the County of Provence was governed by the Counts of Barcelona. The most famous of these, Raimond-Bérenger V (1209-1245), was known throughout Europe both for his legislative achievements and the gallantry of his court which was extolled in song by the troubadours. Of his four daughters, the first married Louis IX of France, better known as St-Louis and in 1246 Béatrix, the youngest, married the French king's brother Charles of Anjou (1226-1285), who became the Count of Provence under the title of Charles 1st.

CORRIDA IN ARLES

Angevin Provence

Charles 1st of Anjou, Count of Provence, founded the Angevin dynasty which was to reign over Provence until it was united with the French crown. In 1266 he conquered the Kingdom of Naples and Sicily, attaching its royal title to that of Provence. Marseille, ever the rebel, refused to recognize his sovereignty and suffered several attacks and sieges before giving up its independence in 1257.

More commercially active than ever, Marseille took full advantage of the expanding maritime trade brought about by the crusades (1096-1270). Marseille ships laden with soldiers, or later with pilgrims travelling to Jerusalem, established trading links with Palestine. From these ports they brought back oranges, lemons, grapes, figs, sugarcane, wines from Gaza, rugs from Damascus, glass ware, purple dyes, gold and silver objects, goods from the Far East, and even slaves. Indian spices, Chinese perfumes, Arabian incense, African ivory and precious stones were brought in by trading caravans. Piled high with the riches of the East, Marseille was an exotic bazaar, a city of seafaring traders which had established its own kingdom on the Mediterranean sea.

Avignon was also to have a separate destiny. From 1305 until 1376 it was the city of the Popes and during the 14th century its prestige was overwhelming. It was Clement V who decided to install the Holy See here, preferring it to Rome which, like the rest of Italy, was suffering periods of violence and insecurity resulting from political unrest. Jean XXII, who succeeded him extended his earthly control over the gold with which he filled the papal coffers. His successors, Benedict XII and Clement VI increased this wealth and used it for the construction of the famous Palais des Papes. Petrarch fulminated in his writings against 'the insolent luxury' of this hive of cardinals and prelates, princes and ambassadors, artists and courtesans. But in addition to the wealth, the Popes also brought to Avignon 'a whole world of artists and craftsmen', who have left us some remarkable achievements of the goldsmith's craft, tapestry, sculpture (including the elaborate effigies on papal tombs), and painting. The latter art developed, as in Italy at the same period, into the early stirrings of Renaissance art.

The second half of the 14th century was to be less happy for other parts of Provence. During the reign of Charles 1st's great-granddaughter, Jeanne, Queen of Naples and Countess of Provence from 1343 to 1382, the County suffered civil war and was ravaged by mercenaries demobilized during the treaties of the Hundred Years' War. The Black Death which spread from Marseille scattered the population and aggravated the famine conditions. During this dark and troubled period Queen Jeanne enjoyed great popularity and her vibrant personality seduced the population. Everyone praised her great beauty and gossiped about her four successive marriages. Her tragic death - she was suffocated at the orders of her heir and cousin, Charles de Duras - is typical of 'political' behaviour in the Middle Ages.

Provence's recovery a century later corresponds with the reign of King René, another great historical figure of the Angevin dynasty. Whether he was a prudent administrator concerned for the welfare of his people, or a 'greedy prince' reaping the fruits of fortunate circumstances, it was above all his love of the arts and sciences which earned him his lasting fame.

French Provence

Provence was bequeathed by King René's heir to King Louis XI of France in 1482, and despite statutory equality with France (which was to continue until 1789), her independence was lost. For three hundred years opposition by Provençal nobility to the royal centralizing power was fairly steady but within this formal stand-off position not only the privileges but also Provence's cultural identity was at risk - the Langue d'Oc versus the Langue d'Oïl. In 1501 Louis XII created a Parliamentary court aimed at strengthening royal authority. In time the Parlement de Provence, Provence's own parliament, run by Provençals, was to play a double role, both political and cultural. This dual culture, both Provençal and French, was centred on Aix and became the focus of claims to independence which would endure until the French Revolution.

During the first half of the 16th century Provence suffered the consequences of the confrontation between François I and Charles V of Spain, nor did she escape the Wars of Religion during the second half of the century; here as elsewhere the strife soon took on all the aspects of a civil war.

The 17th and 18th centuries were a golden age, evident in an artistic flowering no longer constrained by religion. The proliferating construction of great private houses, *hôtels particuliers*, in Aix-en-Provence, Arles and Tarascon encouraged the blossoming of secular architecture, first Baroque then Classical in style.

The French Revolution brought fresh outbreaks of violence in Provence. The region was distinguished in national history by its tempestuous representative at the States General, Mirabeau, and in 1792 by its popular delegation which joined in the assault on the Tuileries to the sounds of the 'Marseillaise'.

In the 19th century Provence was divided up into *départements* and lost its unified identity. The 'restoration' of the Occitan language by the writer Frédéric Mistral has no real roots in 20th century attitudes either.

The large cities, centres of university education, of trade or of culture exercise a growing attraction over the rest of the county and in summer the cosmopolitan population gravitates around numerous festivals. The true spirit of Provence has fled to the small towns which are happily still largely ignored by the developers.

THE ARTISTIC HERITAGE

ARCHITECTURE FROM CLASSICAL TIMES TO THE 18TH CENTURY

Over 600 years of Roman occupation has left many monuments in Provence, at Glanum, Vaison-la-Romaine, Arles and Orange, for example. In some cases their beauty rivalling remains in Italy.

Glanum was the predecessor of St-Rémy-de-Provence, established to the south of the Gallo-Roman city after it was destroyed by the barbarians in 270 AD. It was not until the early 20th century that large-scale excavations exposed the buried town and three superimposed layers of construction were discovered: Celto-Ligurian, Hellenist (the influence of Massalia), and finally Roman, from the period of the 'provincia romana'.

Characteristically Greek in its square lay-out, the House of Antes lies round a central court with peristyle. In the House of Atys and Cybele, which was modified in Roman times, the peristyle has been turned into a shrine dedicated to the goddess Cybele, while a second building was laid out round an atrium. The House of Capricorn, near the baths, and the House of Sulla, beneath the Forum, have revealed very fine mosaics. The treasures dug up at this site are on display in the Hôtel de Sade archaeological centre in St-Rémy. Also in Glanum lie "Les Antiques", two magnificent Roman monuments from the end of the 1st century BC. The arch, which has lost its upper part, has superb carved motifs commemorating the Roman conquest of Gaul. The remarkably well-preserved mausoleum stands on a square plinth with four carved bas-reliefs. A conical roof carved like fish scales concludes the design.

The modern town of Vaison-la-Romaine is built over substantial Roman remains which were discovered in the two outlying districts of Villasse and Puymin. The archaeological museum nearby contains statues, mosaics and objects found during the excavations.

A Roman colony by the 1st century BC, Arles attained the height of its prestige during the 4th century AD when the poet Ausonius described it - with slight exaggeration - as 'The Gaulish Rome': its Roman theatre, the cryptoporticus (the substructure of the Forum), the Roman arena and the baths of Constantine's Palace constitute the town's greatest treasures from ancient times, with fresh excavations constantly adding to this wealth. The remains of the Augustan theatre (1st century BC), almost entirely destroyed in the 5th century, were discovered during the 19th century. At 136m long by 107m broad, the amphitheatre, dating from the 1st century AD and known as Les Arènes, is the largest classical edifice in the whole of Provence; two of its original three storeys still exist, each with 60 open arcades. The three towers on the summit of the building date from the Middle Ages. Restored in the 19th century, the amphitheatre has now returned to its original appearance and purpose, with bull fights taking place in the arena. The Baths (Les Thermes), a later construction, date from Arles's golden age of classicism, the 4th century AD. Beyond the great hall of the hot baths (the caldarium), the very beautiful semi-circular apse which contained the swimming pool is built of stone and brick beneath a half dome. The Museum of Pagan Art contains many statues and mosaics from local excavations: the Altar of Apollo and the sarcophagus known as the tomb of Phaedra and Hippolytus are among its most remarkable items.

Orange, another important Roman colony in classical times, still has its ancient theatre, a splendid monument which is particularly well preserved. Unique throughout the Mediterranean world, including Italy, it still has its original façade, 103m long by 36m high, and the entire back wall of the stage. Standing alone and restored in the 19th century, this theatre still has remarkable acoustic qualities: restored to use in 1869, since 1970 it has been used as an opera centre, the annual 'Chorégies' festival famous throughout the world. The Triumphal Arch, commemorating the foundation of the Roman colony in 20 AD is heavily decorated with carvings celebrating the Roman army.

To see the most impressive example of a Roman aqueduct bridge, you have to leave Provence by crossing its natural frontier, the River Rhône. The Pont du Gard, built towards the end of the 1st century BC, consists of three levels, decreasing in width from bottom to top. The six arches at the lowest level, eleven in the centre and thirty-five at the top make up an edifice as harmonious as it is vast, being 49m high and 275m long. The great dressed-stone blocks are trimmed to fit snugly against or on top of each other in the Greek style, without mortar or cement.

For lovers of classical history an expedition to Nîmes offers another opportunity to see an amphitheatre (arena), an Augustan temple (the Maison Carré), and the adjacent museums of antiquities and archaeology.

Romanesque Art

The growing wealth of the Church and the rediscovery of classical art at the end of the 11th century brought fresh architectural energy to Provence. Provençal Romanesque art reached its peak in the 12th century, and from small churches up to cathedrals there are characteristic features such as the single nave, the barrel vaulting - with semi-circular or pointed arches - the narrow openings and the octagonal cupola above the transept crossing between the nave and the choir. The simplicity of the design of these buildings allied to sober decoration often classically inspired, bestows on them a great and pure beauty.

In the *département* of the Bouches-du-Rhône, St-Trophime in Arles, rebuilt at the end of the 11th century and the first half of the 12th century, was embellished around 1190 with a magnificent and richly decorated portico, emphasising the impressive plainness of the rest of the building. The no less famous cloister has four arcades surrounding a rectangular court; those to the north and east are Romanesque (late 12th century), while those to the south and west are Gothic (14th century). Like the porch, the Romanesque arcades are decorated with numerous carvings. Among some remarkable decorative works inside the church there are 17th-century Aubusson tapestries in the nave and paintings by the great 17th-century Bruges master

THE ARENES, ARLES

Finsonius; the Chapel of the Kings has an *Adoration of the Magi*, there is a *Stoning of St-Stephen* in the choir, and an *Annunciation* in the left transept.

Sloping land near Arles inspired an unusual design for the Abbey of Notre-Dame de Montmajour, where in the mid-12th century the architects placed one church on top of another: the lower church, or crypt, half hollowed out of the rock, created the necessary level foundation for the upper church. Almost as big as the church itself, the square cloister (late 12th and early 13th century) lies next to the south side of the church, the carvings on the capitals and the plinths of its columns reminiscent in style of those at St-Trophime.

Other notable buildings in the *département* are the Chapel of St-Gabriel near Les Baux, the St-Sauveur cloister at Aix-en-Provence, and the Vieille Major cathedral in Marseille.

In the *département* of Vaucluse: the church of Notre-Dame-du-Lac at Le Thor, near L'Isle-sur-Sorgue, was built in the late 12th century and is one of the most beautiful in Vaucluse. It has all the traditional features: a single nave, octagonal cupola above the choir and classical-style decoration.

Although the cathedral of Notre-Dame-des-Doms in Avignon has been enlarged and modified down the centuries, it retains various characteristic features of the high Romanesque period of its construction (1140-1160), such as the antique-style portico and the cupola lantern tower. Statues and paintings from all ages bring together the work of some prestigious artists: frescoes by Simone Martini (14th century), paintings by the 17th-century artists Nicolas and Pierre Mignard, carved 17th-century silver figures by Pierre Puget, and 19th-century pictures by Eugène Devéria.

Other important Romanesque buildings in this *département* include the former cathedral of Notre-Dame-de-Nazareth at Vaison-la-Romaine; the church of Ste-Marie-St-Véran at Fontaine-de-Vaucluse; the chapel of St-Symphorien at Caumont-sur-Durance; and the priory church of St-Christol-d'Albion.

Church architecture in the *département* of Haute-Provence is divided between Rhône valley influence and the more alpine type of Romanesque construction. The cathedral of Notre-Dame-des-Pommiers at Sisteron was built at the end of the 12th century on the remains of a former classical necropolis. In basilica style it has three naves ending in three apses. Lombard influence is noticeable in the dichromatic portico and apse, and particularly in the octagonal cupola, near the bell-tower, with pretty colonnettes.

Perched on the plateau of the same name, near Lurs, the Benedictine priory church of Ganagobie is one of the undoubted masterpieces of Provençal Romanesque art. Founded in the 10th century, the priory gained greatly in wealth during the 12th and 13th centuries under the protection of the Counts of Forcalquier. The church was built during this period of prosperity, in the middle of the 12th century. Inside, the sanctuary floor has exceptionally fine mosaics: geometrical forms, fantastic animals (elephants, griffons, centaurs, etc), biblical scenes (St-George slaying the dragon), all laid out in three main colours, black, white and red. The design of the late 12th-century cloister is reminiscent of that of Montmajour.

Other notable Romanesque buildings in the *département* include Notre-Dame-de-Salagon, the church of St-Donat and the cathedral of Notre-Dame-du-Bourg at Digne.

Three abbeys merit special mention: Sénanque (Vaucluse), Silvacane (Bouches-du-Rhône) and Le Thoronet (Var), known as the 'three Cistercian sisters of Provence'. Plain buildings in quiet places, bare of all ornamentation, they are models of spirituality expressed in stone and given full splendour by the effects of light contained within their interior volume. Built in the late 12th and early 13th centuries, these churches are cruciform in design, the nave flanked with side aisles with barrel-vaulting or pointed arches and ending in an apse with its two apsidal chapels.

The façade of the abbey of St-Gilles (Gard) on the other side of the Rhône is very similar in design

CHATEAU DE TARASCON

to the porch of St-Trophime in Arles: it has the same 'triumphal arch' design and profusely ornamented portico. Dating from the middle of the 12th century, it would appear to have inspired St-Trophime's architect.

Gothic Art

The pointed-arch vaulting in religious architecture was replaced in the 13th century by intersecting ribbed vaults; buttresses and the single nave design continued, however, while the builders of northern France preferred flying buttresses and cruciform design. Civil and military architecture of this period can be seen in the château at Tarascon, the fortifications at Pernes-les-Fontaines, and above all in the magnificent Palais des Papes in Avignon. This city was both a brilliant artistic centre and the birthplace of a famous school of painting.

The Palais des Papes, the jewel of the city of Avignon, was built between 1335 and 1358. The section known nowadays as the Old Palace (the northern half), was built by Benedict XII, the third Avignon pope. It is as large as an entire town, as strongly fortified as a fortress and as austere as a cloister. His successor, Clement VI, was a pope of a different style and in order to house and support his court - one of the most elegant in Europe - he built what is now known as the New Palace, the southern section, resplendent with all Gothic luxuries. On the outside the turrets with cut-off sections and the corner tower softened the solid and warlike appearance of the adjoining Old Palace. The artists Simone Martini and then Matteo Giovanetti were appointed to decorate the interior.

Other significant Gothic buildings in Avignon are the churches of St-Pierre (14th-16th centuries) and St-Agricol (rebuilt in the 15th century), the Petit Palais (14th-15th centuries) and the 14th-century Livrée Ceccano, now the municipal library, with painted ceilings and heraldic frescoes.

The earliest buildings of the Carthusian monastery of Le Val-de-Bénédiction at Villeneuve-lès-Avignon were constructed for the future Pope Innocent VI, then a cardinal. The 14th-century church contains his tomb (1362), constructed in marble and Pernes stone by Barthélemy Cavalier. The pontifical chapel is decorated with frescoes painted by Matteo Giovanetti, the Pope's court painter.

Perched on a rock beside the River Rhône, the château of King René at Tarascon was completely rebuilt on the foundations of an earlier château between 1400 and 1435 and furnished and decorated between 1447 and 1449 for the king. From the exterior the château is austerely martial with four massive towers, but the flamboyant Gothic elegance of the seigneurial residential portion is visible from the central court of honour.

The former capital of the Comtat Venaissin, Pernes-les-Fontaines still has impressive fortified gates dating from the 15th and 16th centuries, remains of the ramparts which were demolished in the 19th century.

The basilica of Ste-Marie-Madeleine at St-Maximin-la-Ste-Baume, built between 1295 and 1316 round the supposed tomb of Mary Magdalene, was enlarged early in both the 15th and 16th centuries. It is acknowledged as Provence's Gothic masterpiece; apart from its impressive size (72m long, 28m high and 37m wide), it skilfully combines the Provençal style with innovation from northern France. The late 4th- and 5th-century crypt contains some classical fragments and carved 5th-century saints' tombs. The former royal convent next to the basilica has a delightful 15th-century cloister abundantly decorated with foliage.

Other impressive religious Gothic buildings include the former cathedral of St-Siffrein, in Carpentras, the cathedral of St-Sauveur in Aix (the central aisle), the basilica of St-Victor in Marseille, and the collegiate church of Ste-Marthe in Tarascon.

The Avignon School

In the history of painting, this was a school with its own particular style; an artistic movement marking a turning-point in the development from Gothic style to the Renaissance, and one that was born in the luxurious court of the Popes, under the influence of Italian artists.

Simone Martini of Sienna and Matteo Giovanetti covered the austere 14th-century Palais des Papes with frescoes, blending brightly contrasting colours inherited from Giotto with a typically Italian suppleness of line.

The following century was dominated by two figures from the north. Enguerrand Quarton (or Charonthon) from the Champagne region introduced Flemish techniques to Avignon: his *Coronation of the Virgin* (1453-54) can be seen in the museum at Villeneuve-lès-Avignon, and the masterpiece known as *The Avignon Pietà* in the Louvre is generally attributed to him, with its sublime harmonies of Italian grace and feeling, dramatic Flemish intensity and French rigour and realism. The same influence and techniques can be seen in the work of Nicolas Froment (1425-1484), known as the 'Van Eyck of Avignon', who became official court painter to King René in 1471. His masterpiece, the triptych of *The Burning Bush*, painted in Avignon in 1474-76, can be seen in the cathedral of St-Sauveur in Aix-en-Provence.

Renaissance Art of the 16th century

Renaissance art enjoyed only a modest flowering in Provence, leaving few outstanding works in a heritage dominated by Romanesque and Gothic religious architecture and by the secular architecture of the 17th and 18th centuries. The Hôtel de Cabre and the Maison Diamanté are two of Marseille's buildings which reveal traces of Renaissance style. The former, built in 1535, is still Gothic in overall design but has Renaissance ornamentation such as cupids. The Maison Diamanté, built and modified between 1570 and 1620, wavers between true Renaissance style and its final stage, Mannerism, which marked the transition to Baroque.

Dominating the attractive village of the same name, the château of Gordes, rebuilt in the 14th and 16th centuries on the site of an earlier fortress, owes its conservation to the 20th-century artist Victor Vasarely; it now contains a museum devoted to his works. On its east and north sides are traces of a fortified castle, while to the south a massive Renaissance façade is flanked by watch-towers and pierced by mullion windows.

The château of Lourmarin is also partly Gothic (the old château, 1495-1525) and partly Renaissance (the new château, mid-16th century). The grand spiral staircase in the latter is unusual in that it ends in a cupola supported by an elegant colonnette.

Further fine Renaissance buildings to see are the Hôtel Mistral de Mondragon at St-Rémy-de-Provence, built around 1550 and now the museum of the Alpilles; the Pavillon de la Reine Jeanne, at the mouth of the Fontaine valley near Les Baux; the Hôtel de Manville, now the Mairie, tourist information office and museum in Les Baux; the remains of the château de la Tour d'Aigues; and the Citadelle de Sisteron.

17th and 18th century Baroque and Classical Art

The combination of an Aix-en-Provence parliamentary nobility avid for prestige and Avignon's prosperity helped to make Provence a flourishing and productive centre of artistic creativity in the 17th and 18th centuries. The ornamental profusion of the 17th-century Baroque style was followed by, and sometimes overlaid with, the austere elegance of the 18th-century classicism.

In Avignon the 18th-century chapelle des Pénitents-Noirs-de-le-Miséricorde yielded to the decorative delights of the Baroque, with its profusion of woodwork and marble to which were added the paintings of Mignard, Parrocel and Levieux. The façades of the large private houses are richly carved: the 17th-century Hôtel des Monnaies; the 1649 Hôtel Berton de Crillon; the modern Calvet Museum, installed in one of the finest 18th-century private houses, retains much of its original interior fittings and décor.

Aix-en-Provence enjoyed a veritable flowering of stylish and luxurious hôtels particuliers or town houses. There are no less than 40 within the thousand square metres of the town centre. The Cours Mirabeau, the carriage avenue created after the mid-17th-century construction of the aristocratic Mazarin quarter, became the city's main street, lined with cafés on the left and banks on the right, and also about a dozen grand town houses. The quartier Mazarin, lying to the south of the Cours Mirabeau, is a pleasant place for strolling, with greenery growing over the high walls of the many large private houses. At its centre is the place des Quatre Dauphines set around the original Italianate fountain of the same name and bordered with fine houses. From here there is a fine view to the church of St-Jean-de-Malte.

Lying at the foot of the Lubéron hills, the château d'Ansouis dominates the rows of village houses climbing the hillside. The northern side of the fortress retains its medieval aspect, but on the south side the regular design of the delicate 16th-century façade proclaims the sober elegance of the Classical style.

The château of Simiane, rebuilt at the end of the 17th and beginning of the 18th centuries, is now the town hall of Valréas.

THE MAJOR MUSEUMS
With its great cultural wealth, Provence has a number of prestigious museums.

Aix-en-Provence
Musée Granet, place St-Jean-de-Malte: open daily except Tues and public holidays, 10-12 and 2-6. Department of archaeology;
Department of painting: works by Cézanne, Philippe de Champaigne, Clouet, David, Granet, Matteo Giovanetti, Greuze, Franz Hals, Ingres, Largillière, Léger, Le Nain, Masson, Parrocel, Rigaud, Rubens, Van Loo.

Avignon
Musée Calvet: open daily except Tues, 10-12 and 2-6.
Gallery of Pre-history;
Gallery of Greek antiquities;
Gallery of iron-work;
Galleries of 16th- and 17th-century painting: works by Louis Le Nain and Pierre and Nicolas Mignard.
Galleries of 17th- and 18th-century painting: works by Forbera, Pierre Parrocel, Hubert Robert, Joseph Vernet, Mme Vigée-Lebrun;
Galleries of 18th- and 19th-century painting: works by Chasseriau, Corot, Daumier, David, Géricault, Manet, Toulouse-Lautrec, Horace Vernet.

Musée du Petit Palais: open daily except Tues and public holidays, 9.15-11.50 and 2-6 in winter, 9.30-11.50 and 2-6.15 in summer.
Italian paintings of the 14th, 15th and 16th centuries.

Marseille
Musée Cantini: 19 rue Grignan, metro station Estrangin-Préfecture: open daily except Tues, Wed morning and public holidays, 10-12 and 2-6.30.
Gallery of Marseille and Provençal (Moustiers) pottery;
Galleries of contemporary art: works by Alechinsky, Arthaud, César, Max Ernst, Ipoustéguy, Magnelli, Masson, Michaux, Miro and Picabia.

Musée des Beaux-Arts: palais Longchamps, metro station Longchamps-Cinq-Avenues; open daily except Tues and Wed morning, 10-12 and 2-6.30.
Gallery Pierre Puget;
Galleries of 16th- and 17th-century painting, with works by Brueghel de Velours, Cariani, Carrache, le Guerchin, Joardens, Largillière, Perugino, Rigaud, Rubens, Michel Serre, Le Sueur, Téniers, Vouet;
Galleries of 18th-, 19th- and 20th-century painting, with works by Corot, Courbet, Daumier, David, Gérard, Girodet, Greuze, Gros, Ingres, Millet, Nattier, Signac, Van Loo, Joseph Vernet, Mme Vigée-Lebrun;
Murals by Puvis de Chavannes in the stair-well;
Gallery of African art.

LITERATURE AND ART

THE GREAT ARTISTS OF THE 19TH AND 20TH CENTURIES

Change in 19th-century Provence was greater and more rapid than at any earlier time. Immigration from nations beyond the Alps and the fascination held by those from other regions of France for the cities of Provence were fostered by improvements in transport. Compulsory education demoted the Provençal language in favour of French, a factor which brought fears for the distinct identity and independence of character which had survived wars and political reforms for so long. Against the tide of history, the artists praised the unique nature of Provence more fervently than ever. The region was seen by the general public as exotic and in time became a major attraction to be exploited by the tourist industry. The modern myth of Provence thrived on the luminous painting of Cézanne and Van Gogh, the tender-hearted poems of writers such as Daudet and Pagnol, or the earthy sensuality of others such as Jean Giono or René Char.

Marseille-born Honoré Daumier (1808-1879) moved to Paris in search of literary glory. There he discovered the 'stupidity, vanity, cruelty and complacency' so well described by his contemporary Honoré de Balzac in *Les Illusions Perdues*. However, this disillusionment stirred into life a talent which was to be the source of his fame as a caricaturist. Like the 18th-century Provençal artist, Pierre Puget, he had several strings to his bow, for he was also a painter and most of all a sculptor of the same acid virulence. Some of his work can be seen in Marseille.

Musée des Beaux-Arts, *open daily except Tues and Wed mornings, 10-12 and 2-6.30.*

Frédéric Mistral (1830-1914) was the standard-bearer of a group of poets known as the Félibrige which in the mid-19th century attempted to preserve the literary vitality and dignity of the Provençal language. His work is concerned with the themes of Provence under threat - its traditions and its language, its nostalgia for a pre-Revolutionary past on a more human scale - expressed by strong attachment to the ordinary humble trades of shepherd, fisherman, craftsman or farmer. His talents brought him a literary fame which spread beyond the movement's political and social framework and which counterbalanced the scorn of the Academicians and the upper bourgeoisie for what they saw as the 'common' Provençal tongue. Broader-minded than his detractors, Mistral himself translated into French his own works originally written in Provençal, including *Mireoi* which became *Mireille*. This movement was also undoubtedly responsible for the preservation of the significant folk heritage passed down in the works of this period and accessible through the collections in the Museon Arlaten founded by Mistral in 1896.

Museon Arlaten, *29 rue de la République, Arles. Open daily, 9-12 and 2-7; closed on Mon, Oct-Jun.*
Museon Mistral, *11 rue Lamartine, Maillane. Open daily, 9-12 and 2-6; closed Mon and holidays.*

Alphonse Daudet (1840-1897), born in Nîmes, is linked with Provençal literature by the same ties which linked him with the Félibrige group, and above all by his friendship with Frédéric Mistral. It was no doubt the latter who opened his eyes to the poetic aspect of Provence, seen at the heart of his famous *Lettres de Mon Moulin, (La Chèvre de M. Seguin, La Mule du Pape),* and his *Contes du Lundi.* It was in this tradition as a story-teller, inspired by the Félibres, that Daudet's greatest achievements can be found; the freshness and 'exoticism' of his texts brought him great success among his Parisian readers. His famous tale of *Tartarin de Tarascon,* on the other hand, did not endear him to the people of Tarascon, who doubtless found the caricature somewhat excessive - but the myth of the boastful indecisive Provençal character was established. Finally, and on a different level of inspiration, there is Daudet's story of *L'Arlesienne,* set to music by Georges Bizet: this is the essence of violent southern passion intoxicated with sun and colour.

Musée Alphonse Daudet, *Moulin de Daudet, Fontvieille: 10-12 and 2-5, Oct-Apr; 9-12 and 2-7, Apr-Sep. Closed in Jan.*

Emile Zola (1840-1902) had no great affection for Aix-en-Provence, the town of his childhood which he later described as 'hypocritical and hostile' and whose countryside he often explored with his friend and fellow creative artist, Paul Cézanne. Once in Paris, however, Zola drew on this background for several novels in his famous *Rougon-Macquart* series, subtitled *Histoire Naturelle et Sociale d'une Famille sous le Second Empire.*

Paul Cézanne (1839-1906) was born into the bourgeoisie of an Aix-en-Provence banking family, and also suffered from the narrow-minded attitudes of a society which saw him throughout life as 'an outcast and an eccentric'. The young Cézanne 'sacrificed everything to art and led a bohemian life'. Although he was one of the exhibiting artists in the first Impressionist exhibition in 1874, he soon turned away from this school of 'ephemeral impressions expressed by changing light conditions.' He preferred instead the 'richness of what is real' and took as his first point of departure the juxtaposition of different colours. Apart from his excellent portraits, *Joueurs de cartes*, and many still-lifes, he was above all the artist of the Mont Ste-Victoire, the subject of nearly sixty of his paintings. His final watercolours of the mountain attain a magical and sublimely poetic simplicity.

Paintings displayed in the **Musée Granet,** *place St-Jean-de-Malte, Aix, daily 10-12 and 2-6; closed Tues from Sep-Jun.*

His studio at **Atelier Paul Cézanne,** *9 avenue Paul Cézanne, Aix, daily 10-12 and 2.30-6; closed Tues and holidays.*

The light and the landscape of Provence attracted many artists from Renoir to Picasso, and including Matisse. The pioneer, the Dutch-born Vincent Van Gogh (1853-1890) who was the forerunner of the Fauves group and the Expressionists, arrived in Arles in 1888. 'The future of modern art lies in the south,' he wrote. The twisted shapes of olive trees and the 'dark flame of the cypresses', the heady sun shining down from an implacably blue sky, the sharp mountain ridges - his brushstrokes gave to everything an air of hallucination as shapes and colours were interpreted through his uneasy

"APPLES AND ORANGES", CEZANNE

and vertiginous inner vision. The artist's crises made him unpopular with the people of Arles who signed a petition leading to his voluntary retreat within the asylum of St-Paul-de-Mausole near St-Rémy-de-Provence.

The author of the famous play *Cyrano de Bergerac*, Edmond Rostand (1868-1918) was born in Marseille. He is Provence's only romantic writer. His was a late romanticism, rooted in a literary movement which had little to do with Provence except perhaps the unfailing spirit, the touchiness and tender irony found in other Provençal writers in different registers. The masterly verbal execution and Cyrano's magnificent long speeches, the famous *tirades,* could only have come from Rostand's pen; his genius was compared to that of Victor Hugo. Although his work was out of fashion for many years, he has found renewed honours in recent days through the cinema. Jean-Paul Rappeneau's film of *Cyrano de Bergerac* (1990) has drawn a new generation to the virtuosity of his writing.

Next to Jean Giono, the writer Henri Bosco (1888-1976) was the writer who has best described the beauty of the landscapes, the violence of the elements and the mysteries of Provençal nature. His home town of Avignon and the surrounding countryside, including the Lubéron, was the favoured setting for his novels. His sensitive and dream-like writing portrays the intimate complicity between man and his surroundings, the wild heathlands or dark woods of the Lubéron or the farms and fields created by human hand. All the poetry of the soil is here, the best-known of his novels bieing *Le Mas Théotime*.

From La Paraïs, his house on the Mont d'Or on the outskirts of Manosque, Jean Giono (1895-1970) looked out over the brown-tiled roofs of the town. A novelist of Haute-Provence, he was born into a humble household and worked in a bank for twenty years before being able to live solely by his writing. Like Mistral he developed a keen dislike for the modernism and industrialization which were spoiling the countryside and reducing all ways of life to standard forms. His inspiration turned towards the mountains of Lure and Triève, the clear air of the high landscapes, to the true wealth of the soil; like

Henri Bosco he described the secret ties between man and nature, the guarantee of true happiness, as natural and necessary as breathing. The author of *Le Hussard sur le Toit* was also a teller of rich and complex fables, creating imaginary worlds which sometimes found a setting in a reinvented version of Provence. This was the prose of the real recreated in poetic style. He wrote:

In Manosque I always intend to walk eastwards so that as I come round the hillside I can see across the cleft of the Durance valley to the great bowl of opaline blue with the enormous sugar lumps which are the Alps. The sight of the glaciers and the chamois pastures is all I need to fire my breath and my blood.

Marcel Pagnol (1895-1974), born in the little town of Aubagne at the foot of the Garlaban hills near Marseille, is unique among the great artistic personalities of modern Provence. A great playwright, he also shared in the creation of the French film industry's Realist tradition from 1929 to 1952 and brought honour to the southern accent. His questionable use of colourful stereotypes, brought to life by the great actors Raimu and Fernandel, is balanced by the profoundly humane and moving aspects of his characters. His memoirs, written towards the end of his life, come close to Daudet's prose in their earthy humour and tenderness.

Provence continues to attract great 20th-century artists. In the wake of Picasso, the artist André Masson (1896-1987), the 'painter with a winged hand 'settled in Le Tholonet near Aix in 1947 and painted a series of Provençal landscapes.

Works on view at the **Musée Granet**, *place St-Jean-de-Malte, Aix: daily 10-12 and 2-6, closed Tues from Sep-Jun.*

Musée Cantini, *19 rue Grignan, Marseille: daily 12-7, closed on public holidays.*

René Char (1907-1988), one of the 20th-century's greatest poets, was born and lived at l'Isle-sur-Sorgue. His poetry, nourished in contemplation of Provence's landscapes and illuminated by its violently contrasting colours, consists of vivid imagery framed in powerfully evocative language giving expression to intense and profound human attitudes.

FOOD AND DRINK

CUISINE DU SOLEIL

Wines of the region
Between Valréas and Avignon, Côtes du Rhône de Vaucluse:

A.O.C.
Côtes du Ventoux: robust reds with a good bouquet, fresh, smooth rosés, lively and well-balanced dry whites.
Châteauneuf du Pape: the most important of the red Côtes du Rhônes, full-bodied, robust, truly 'heady'.
Gigondas: red wine very similar to Châteauneuf du Pape, but smoother and more lively to drink.

V.D.N.
Rasteau: produces a sweet wine and Les-Baumes-de-Venise a Muscadet, both of which are dessert wines.

Between the Lubéron and the Mediterranean area of the Provence appellation:

A.O.C.
Reds, rosés and whites; renowned whites, robust, smooth and with a good bouquet.
Cassis: Reds, rosés and whites; excellent dry, fragrant, robust and heady whites; full-bodied and robust reds.
Bandol: excellent but scarce reds; rosés should be drunk young; fresh smooth whites with a good bouquet.
The Côtes de Provence (classified A.O.C. since 1978) account for 80% of the appellation Provence; although very pleasant, they rarely attain the heights of the three great *crus* listed above.

V.D.Q.S.
Côteaux d'Aix: fresh, fruity reds, dry whites with a good bouquet, stylish rosés.
Côtes du Lubéron: reds, rosés and whites; smooth, fresh and light; should be drunk young.

Provençal gastronomy developed as a result of an abundance of local produce. From Orange to Carpentras, from Châteaurenard to Cavaillon and Avignon is known as the 'garden of France' where nearly 20% of the nations's fruit and vegetables are grown. Var is the largest fig producer in the country; and the tenderness of the Arles Merinos and lamb from the Alpilles and Sisteron regions are much vaunted. Every day the Mediterranean yields its harvest of fish and shellfish. Olive and almond trees dispute the territory of the hillsides with grape vines. Truffles are found in the north-east, the much sought after 'black diamonds', and the Camargue is the kingdom of rice. Here too, where you would not believe anything could grow, can be seen fragrant carpets of thyme, sage, savory, rosemary, mint, basil, hyssop, fennel and tarragon all culled to enrich everyday cookery.

In the Camargue, rice is used as an important addition to tomatoes, onions and aubergines - the vegetables most typical of Provence. They are found in *catigot d'anguilles,* a kind of eel stew with red wine, onions, tomatoes, celery and bay leaf. This dish is found too in Martigues, where garlic replaces the onion. This ancient fishing port has long been famous for its *poutargue.* Made of salt cod's roe presented in a flat sausage shape it is known as 'white caviar'.

Many variations of the famous *bouillabaisse* (fish soup) exist. In Martigues it may be made only with mullet or with cuttlefish (it then becomes *bouillabaisse noire*). In Marseille it is basically made with fish from the rocks, such as conger eel, gurnard and sea bass. Reboul, in his *Provençal Cookery* (1895), lists over 40 kinds of fish used in *bouillabaisse* - in other words you can put in any fish your fishmonger stocks. Its specific flavour comes from the tomatoes, onions, saffron, olive oil and *rouille, a* garlic and pimento sauce.

Bourride is another variation on fish soup, softened by strained vegetables and with the saffron

INGREDIENTS FOR "BOUILLABAISSE"

THE MARKET AT CARPENTRAS

and *rouille* replaced by *aïoli*, an egg yolk, oil and garlic sauce. Calamari, squid, sea urchins, oysters and clams are also good in *bourride*. A variety of small shellfish, including mussels, cockles and tiny crabs are delicious on many fresh pasta dishes brought to France through the port of Marseille. Between Marseille and Martigues, Carry is renowned for its cream of sea urchin soup and Le Rouet for its goat's milk cheese called *brousse*. Marseille is also the production centre of France for pastis, alcohol made with aniseed. In Provence, pastis is more than an aperitif, more even than a tradition, practically an institution.

The speciality of Aix-en-Provence is the famous *calisson*, almond paste sweet biscuits. There are many traditional recipes from this region, such as *soupe au pistou* originating, like pasta, from Genoa and made basically with beans, various vegetables and pasta, flavoured with garlic and basil. Beef is used here in *pot au feu* or *daube* and every Friday butchers make quantities of aïoli, a garlic mayonnaise served also with cold fish and boiled vegetables. In traditional bakeries *pompe à huiles*, flat coronets of bread flavoured with olive oil are still to be found. These are also called *gibassiers*. *Fougasses* is another variety of flavoured bread made with nuts, olives and sometimes small pieces of bacon. Country biscuits like *chichi fregi* (in little sticks) or *oreillettes* a kind of doughnut are found also in Marseille and Arles.

Arles is proud of its famous *saucisson d'Arles*, a beef and pork sausage and of its Merino sheep grazed on the plains of Crau in winter and the mountain pastures in the summer. As in Sisteron they boast of the tenderness and flavour of their lamb, enhanced by herbs or garlic. In Arles as in Avignon mutton is preferred to beef for stewing.

From Avignon to Carpentras they make *tian*, a vegetable gratin with meat, fish or eggs. Carpentras is also the business capital of the truffle, harvested in Provence on the Valensole plateau and on the slopes of Mont Ventoux, and used in numerous dishes. Apt is the headquarters of crystallized fruits, a taste enjoyed by popes in the 14th century. Between Lure and Lubéron is Banon, a modest village which gave birth to the famous goat's cheese which bears its name. This is flavoured with savory and may be recognized by its distinctive chestnut-leaf wrapping.

Gastronomy and tradition are still inextricably linked, many dishes invoking the religious calendar which in former times was scrupulously observed: aïoli was reserved for Ash Wednesday and leg of lamb traditionally eaten on Easter Sunday. The little boat-shaped biscuits made for Candlemas or the thirteen Christmas sweets; dried raisins and dried figs, almonds and nuts, plums and dates, pears and apples, crystallized lemon and quince, black nougat with almonds and *calissons* are typical examples of these.

Markets in Provence
"Here is the noble bay and the wild thyme ..." Celebrated in song by Gilbert Becaud, the markets of Provence are an image of the region: sunny and colourful both in the produce on sale and in their reigning atmosphere.

Lit by the sweet sunshine of early morning and depending on the season of the year, the display of fine red tomatoes may accompany fennel bulbs, asparagus, aubergines, Cavaillon melons, and all the fruits of the south - cherries, peaches, nectarines and apricots.

Spring and autumn bring wonderful fungi - morels, agaric, ceps and field mushrooms, and truffles in the Comtat Venaissin and the Lubéron regions.

There is more here than fresh fruit and vegetables - we are all familiar with the famous strings of garlic bulbs plaited together, black or green olives offered for sale *à la Provençale* and olive oil. Nor should we forget Avignon sausages, goat cheeses from Haute-Provence (particularly the famous Banon), nougat, pralines and almond paste.

The range of honeys is equally extensive. Flavoured with lavender, rosemary, chestnut, pine or heather, there is something for all tastes.

More than one-third of France's flowers come from Provence, and naturally some are available in the markets. A whole stall may be dedicated to lavender; dried and sold in little sachets, dressed up as dolls, as essence and as perfume.

Provence means also the Mediterranean and its fish. Fish means the market in the Vieux Port, Marseille's old port: there are sardines (according to legend, a sardine once blocked up the harbour), scorpion fish, bream, sea perch, John Dory - all are offered for sale by the fishermen themselves. For here, more frequently than elsewhere, the 'producers' also distribute their produce; or at least are closely involved. And their lively chat (with local accent) with their customers and the arguments between traders take on a savour all its own. Add to this the range of colour and scents, and you will appreciate the characteristic atmosphere of Provence's markets.

As well at the traditonal markets, all the towns and villages have craft fairs, bric-à-brac fairs, and above all *santons* fairs (particularly along the Canebière in Marseille) for the traditional Christmas crib.

Incidentally, there is no need to go to the markets for your Provence herbs: you need only to bend down and pick them.

LEISURE ACTIVITIES

The following pages cover the prime holiday pursuits visitors to Provence might like to enjoy. In a region where the sun beats ceaselessly for the majority of the year, staying close to the cool of the water is not surprisingly the popular choice. A wide variety of watersports is available; everything from sailing and windsurfing to canal cruising, canoeing and white-water rafting.

While the keen golfer is well provided for with lush fairways situated amidst oak and pine, olives and vines, it is the rough terrain of the Provençal hinterland which beckons the mountain-biking enthusiast and horse rider.

Finally the detailed sections on walking and motoring tours invite you to explore the magnificent scenery of mountain landscape or Mediteranean coastline at your own pace.

LEFT ARLESIAN COSTUME

Loisirs Accueil

For the holidaymaker who is seeking something different, the Loisirs Accueil organization offers unusual and interesting short break ideas, activities varying between the cultural and the sporting; accommodation is also arranged in local gîtes, hotels or camp sites. Contact the following office for futher information:
Loisirs Accueil Bouches-du-Rhône
Domaine du Vergon, 13370 Mallemort
☎ *90.59.18.05*

SPORTS

Practical information on the following popular sports and activities can be obtained direct from the addresses given below.

Aerial Sports
Plein Air Nature
42 boulevard Victor Hugo
Digne-les-Bains
Canoeing/Kayaking
Fédération Française de Canoe-Kayak
B.P. 58, 94340 Joinville-le-Pont
☎ *(1) 48.89.39.89*

Cycling
Fédération Française de Cyclotourisme
8 rue Jean-Marie Jego, 75013 Paris
Fishing
Conseil Supérieure de la Pêche
134 avenue de Malakoff, 75016 Paris
For fishing purposes, French waters are classified into category 1 (for salmon and trout) and category 2 (for all other fish). Local regulations from the Tourist Offices.
Golf
Fédération Française de Golf
689 avenue Victor-Hugo, 75116 Paris
Riding
Direction Nationale pour le Tourisme Equestre (DNTE)
170 quai de Stalingrad,
parc de l'Ile St-Germain
92130 Issy-les-Moulineaux
☎ *(1) 42.54.29.54*
Walking
Fédération Française de Randonné Pédestre
9 avenue George V
75008 Paris
☎ *(1) 47.23.62.32*

FESTIVALS AND TRADITIONS

JOIE DE VIVRE

Many *fêtes* celebrate, and were inspired by, the traditions relating to the trades and occupations found in this region. In the Bas-Rhône area (Arles), bullfights and bull fighting games, such as snatching the cockade from between the bull's horns, are games of skill derived from the arts of branding and breaking practised in stock-rearing areas.

In mountain areas such as the Alpilles, the Christmas *pastrages* or shepherds' festivals, are descended from the Medieval 'Mystery plays' of religious origin, kept alive in the 19th century by pastoral plays. To the music of fife and tambourine, shepherds and shepherdesses in traditional costume bring the offering of a new-born lamb, carried on a cart pulled by a white ram and decorated with ribbons.

Since Provence is also a wine- and olive-producing region as well as an agricultural one, festive traditions linked to the cycle of the grape, the olive and the fields are still common.

BULL RACING, ST-REMY-DE-PROVENCE

POPULAR TRADITIONS

The Christmas crib

This tradition appears to go back to the Middle Ages but was revived in the 18th century when the Carmelites at Aix and Arles made little wax or cardboard figures, in the traditional religious manner. These depicted figures from the Nativity and the Life of Christ and were painted with oil paint. Local figures, such as an Arlesian girl and the tambourine player gradually crept into these scenes adding a local touch. Mostly the cribs are displayed in showcases in churches over the festive period. These figurines enjoy great success with the public and the potters of Apt and Moustiers make porcelain versions which sell far from Provence.

Santons

The craft of making *santons* or statuettes has refined and diversified since the start of the 19th century when the first clay figures appeared, shelack-painted moulded figurines. Around the nativity scene began to appear new characters, intended for family cribs and popular purchase. These figures represented traditional trades: the shepherd, the fisherman, the baker, the blacksmith, the fishmonger, the milkman and the tambourine girl. The first *santon* fair took place in Marseille in 1803 and was soon followed by numerous others.

Pastoral Plays

'Mystery plays' acting out scenes from the old and new testaments, would appear, judging by their success in Provence between the 14th and 17th centuries, to be the forerunners of the pastoral play. In the middle of the 17th century, Nicolas Saboly composed the *Noëls Provençaux*, written texts to be sung and incorporating popular characters appearing simultaneously in the crib scenes. In 1760 the abbot of Gemenos wrote the first 'pastoral play'. Others followed, intended to bring to life nativity scenes and to be performed in churches. Provençal accent and vivacity enlivened these little scenes where popular inspiration is mixed with religion. The inclusion of local characters, such as the *'boumian'* (Arles) and the *'pistachié'* added colour and helped to emphasize local involvement.

Pétanque

Pétanque is derived from an 18th-century game in which balls of different sizes were used on a huge and rough pitch. Today

PROVENCAL SANTON

identically-sized balls are used for the various games. Long boules, played over a 15 to 20 metre length pitch is known more succinctly as *pétanque*, and is played standing still (*pied tanco*). The elements of the game involve 'aiming' (bowling the boule as close as possible to the jack) or 'striking' (dislodging your adversary's boule) and games are the subject of interminable concentration and discussion.

Water jousts
These competitive nautical tournaments take place in various ports along the coast. Two combatants, equipped with shield and lance, perch on a narrow platform on the prow of boats manoeuvred by oarsmen.

Bullfighting games
These have been common for centuries in the Bas-Rhône area. The *course à la cocarde* is practised in the Camargue region, the prize being a plume of feathers plucked daringly by the *razeteur* from between the bull's horns. This is the principle of such competitions as the 'golden cockade' fought for every year in the arena at Arles.

PETANQUE

WATER-JOUSTS, ISTRES

EVENTS WORTH NOTING

Provence, with more than a hundred and fifty music, opera, theatre and dance festivals, is in summer, the centre for French national artistic events.

The oldest of these, the Chorégies d'Orange takes place in the Roman arena and dates back to 1869 and has, since 1970, has been devoted to the lyric arts.

In 1947 the great man of French theatre, Jean Vilar, produced the first "arts week" in Avignon which was to turn into the dramatic arts festival of today. Since 1967 it has included dance and music and the festival takes place in many scenic sites as well as the prestigious courtyard of the Palais des Papes. In addition to the official festival, during the last three weeks of July, much fringe street theatre takes place.

One year later than the birth of the Avignon festival came the Aix-en-Provence festival of lyric art. Originally intended to promote youthful talent, it popularized lesser-known Mozart operas in the 1950s. Four operas are performed each summer in the courtyard of the Archbishop's palace, which since 1985 has benefited from a new stage.

Recent festivals include the Salon-de-Provence jazz festival in the superb setting of the Empéri château and, since 1970, the international Arles photography festival which each summer enlivens the town with numerous exhibitions and events popular with both professional and amateur artists.

BOUCHES-DU-RHONE
Allauch: traditional Provençal Christmas crib and night vigil; Provençal fête in honour of St-Jean (end June)
Arles: Rice harvest festival (September)
Feria Pascale, bullfights (Easter)
Fête des Gardians, cowboys (end April to end May)
Courses à la Cocarde (July, August, September)
Exhibition of *santons* (December)
Berre l'Etang: festival of folklore (mid June to end July)
Les Baux: traditional Provençal Christmas and shepherds' festival (Christmas)
Boulbon: bottle procession (beginning of June)
Carry le Rouet: sea urchin month (February)
Cassis: wine festival (early September)
Fontvieille: shepherds' offering (Christmas)
Graveson: carnival procession (Mardi Gras); feast of St-Eloi (end July)
Istres: celebration of the transhumance,

FEAST OF ST-JEAN, MARSEILLE

moving animals to summer pasturing, and shepherds' festival (mid December)
Marseille: boules competition (end July to early August)
Santons fair (December)
Château Gombert folklore festival (first fortnight in July)
Martigues: Venetian fêtes (early July) folklore festival (first week in August)
Mouriès: olive festival (end September)
La Ste-Baume: St-Madeleine's day fêtes (21 and 22 July)
Les Saintes-Maries-de-la-Mer: gypsies' pilgrimage (end May and end October)
Tarascon: festival of the Tarasque, folk procession and bullfights (end June)

Festivals
Aix-en-Provence: festival of dance (early July); international festival of lyric art (second fortnight in July)
Arles: dance, music, opera and theatre

GYPSY PILGRIMAGE, STES-MARIES-DE-LA-MER

festival (end June to end July)
international photography festival (second week in July)
Marseille: Soirées Borély, lyric art and theatre (mid July); festival of the isles, theatre (end July, mid August)
Martigues, Port-de-Bouc and Saint-Mitre: popular theatre, music, dance exhibitions and festival (second fortnight in July)
Martigues: festival of chamber music (second fortnight in August)
Roque d'Anthéron: international piano festival (August)
Saint-Michel-du-Frigolet: Provençal arts festival (first fortnight in July)
Saint-Rémy-de-Provence: "Organa" festival, organ concerts (July, August, first fortnight in September); jazz festival (third week in July)
Les Stes-Maries-de-la-Mer: Vaccarès theatre (July, August)
Salon-de-Provence, Cassis and St-Martin-de-Crau: Mediterranean festival (early July to end August)
Salon-de-Provence: Jazz festival (third week in July)
Salon and region: Empéri theatre evenings
Tarascon: international contemporary poetry readings (early August)

VAR
Barjols: Fêtes des tripettes: a whole ox is roasted in the village square (once every four years, mid January, 90,94 etc)
Bandol: wine festival (early December); festival of folklore (mid July to mid August)
Beausset: festival of folklore (second week in August)
Ollioules: flower festival (May)
Toulon: fishermen's festival (July)

Festivals
Hyères: jazz festival (end July)
Seyne-sur-Mer: French-speaking

contemporary theatre (July)
Toulon: music festival (June and early July)

VAUCLUSE
Apt: exhibition of *santons* (December)
Bollène: Provençal festival (early September)
Carpentras: truffle market (Jan, Feb and March); St-Siffrein's fair (27 November); night procession (mid July)
Caromb: wine festival (early August)
Cavaillon: bullfighting Saturdays (July and August); feast of the Ascension (May); St-Véran's fair (around 11 November)
Châteauneuf du Pape: fête de la Veraison (early August)
Châteaurenard: St-Eloi's cart, (Saracen-style harness competition) and bull racing (early July); Ste-Madeleine's day - procession of flower decorated farm carts (early August)
Courthézon: vine roots festival (early June)
Coustellet: wine harvest (end September)
Isle-sur-Sorgue: regatta and Provençal market (end July)
Malaucène: summer festival and horse fair (early August)
Monteux: St-Jean's fancy dress fête (around 15 May); St-Jean's famous fireworks display (end August)
Nyons: olive festival (mid July)
Richerenche (Valréas area): truffle mass (January)
Roussillon: ochre and colour festival (Ascension day)
Séguret: Provençal and wine festival (end August); Christmas vigil and pastoral play (Christmas)
Vaison-la-Romaine: procession (Pentecost)
Valréas: St-Jean's night (23 June); lavender night festival (early August)

Festivals
Apt: theatre evenings (mid July to mid August)
Avignon: festival of dramatic art (last three weeks of July)
Carpentras: festival of theatre, lyric art and dance (mid July to early August)

ANCIENT THEATRE FESTIVAL, VAISON-LA-ROMAINE

GARDIAN, ARLES

Fontaine-de-Vaucluse, L'Isle-sur-Sorgue, Lagnes, Saumane and Le Thor: La Sorgue music, theatre and dance festival (July)
La Tour d'Aigues: south Lubéron festival (end June to mid August)
Orange: Chorégies festival, opera and symphonic concerts (early July to end August)
Séguret: Provençal festival (third week in August)
Vaison-la-Romaine: music, theatre and dance festival (early July, early August) choral festival (first fortnight in August, 3 yearly 1989, 1992, 1995 etc)
Valréas: musical evenings (early July to mid August); theatrical evenings (mid July to end August)

GARD
Villeneuve-lès-Avignon: St-Marc wine festival (end April)

Festivals
Aigues-Mortes: festival of dramatic art (end July to mid August)
Villeneuve-lès-Avignon: international summer music, theatre and dance gatherings in the Charterhouse (July to August)

HAUTE-PROVENCE
Festivals
Château Arnoux: jazz festival (July)
Digne-les-Bains: song festival (end July); women's film festival (end September)
Forcalquier (and other locations): Haute Provence music gatherings (early July); festival of summer theatre (end July)
Lincel: Lubéron folk stories night (early July)
Manosque: jazz festival (second fortnight in July)
Simiane-la-Rotonde: music evenings in the Rotunda (early July and early August)

WATERSPORTS

AFLOAT BENEATH THE SUN

Whether by sea, river or lake, Provence offers the opportunity to attempt or perfect the watersport of your choice in one of the most outstanding natural settings of France. Each tiny port, each lake and artificial expanse of water boasts sailing and windsurfing schools and craft for hire. The fast-flowing rivers of the mountainous hinterland offer an increasing choice of white-water sports for the adventurous, while a more leisurely pace of life can be enjoyed by cruising the inland waterways.

NATURAL AND MAN-MADE LAKES

Inland, the *département* of Alpes-de-Haute-Provence offers outstanding watersports facilities. More than 6,000 hectares of lake and stretches of water on the rivers Verdon, Ubaye and Durance are available for Optimist sailing, keelboard craft, windsurfing, Quillard and catamaran. Organizers are generally clubs offering half- or full-day courses over a period of two or three weeks. Apart from basic equipment (board or keelcraft), life jackets are provided and must be worn. Wet suits can also be supplied. These bases often also hire windsurfing boards by the hour, half-day, full-day or longer.

ALPES-DE-HAUTE-PROVENCE
Responsible for promoting the *département's* watersports. Full information available on request.
Association Alpes-de-Haute-Provence
Sports Nautiques
13 rue du Docteur Romieu, B.P. 216
04003 Digne-les-Bains
☎ *92.32.25.32*

Useful addresses of watersport organizations :
❶ Société Nautique de Sainte-Croix-du-Verdon (Verdon)
04550 Ste-Croix-du-Verdon
☎ *92.74.57.94*
❶ Association Voile et Nautisme 04 (Verdon)
04500 Ste-Croix-du-Verdon
☎ *92.77.76.51*
❷ Club Nautique d'Esparron de Verdon
04500 Esparron de Verdon
☎ *92.77.15.25*
❸ Ubaye Lautharet Plein Air Nautisme (Ubaye)
04570 St-Vincent Les Forts
☎ *92.85.53.77*
(access to Lake Serre-Ponçon)
❹ Club Nautique de Castillon (Verdon)
04170 St-Julien du Verdon
☎ *91.89.10.44*
❺ Société Nautique de Château-Arnoux (Durance)
04160 Château-Arnoux
☎ *92.64.19.53*

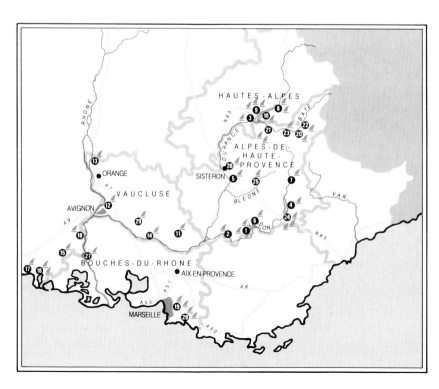

WATERSPORTS, SAGNES LAKE

❻ La Cadeno
04360 Moustiers-Ste-Marie
☎ *92.74.60.85*
❼ Saint-Michel Pleine Nature (Haut-Verdon)
04170 Thorame Haute
☎ *92.83.27.72*

HAUTES-ALPES
Lake Serre-Ponçon is used by several organizations.
❽ Club Nautique Alpin
base de Chadenas
05200 Embrun
☎ *92.43.00.02*
❽ Base de Boscodon-Crots
05200 Embrun
☎ *92.43.35.21*
❾ Auberge de Jeunesse
05160 Savines-le-Lac
☎ *92.44.20.16*
❿ Club Nautique de Chanteloube
05230 Chorges
☎ *92.50.61.08*
❾ Ecole de Voile de l'Encre Bleue
05160 Savines-le-Lac
☎ *92.44.24.36*
❾ Centre de Plein Air les Eygoines
05160 Savines-le-Lac
☎ *92.51.07.91*

VAUCLUSE
⓫ Apt: 10-hectare stretch of water.
Departmental centre of introduction to watersports, open air and leisure base, accommodation.
Route de Saint-Saturnin-d'Apt
84490 Saint-Saturnin
☎ *90.74.50.49*
⓬ Avignon: 125-hectare stretch of water linked to the Rhône (Plan d'eau de Courtine).
Sailing school (craft up to 7 metres), windsurfing, water-skiing, rowing, motor-boating:
Courtine Club
☎ *90.86.41.75*

⓭ Bollène: 25-hectare "Trop Long" stretch of water, windsurfing.
Association des Sociétés Utilisatrices du Plan d'Eau (association of clubs using the stretch of water)
Mairie de Bollène
84500 Bollène
☎ *90.30.97.33*
⓮ Sanne: 33-hectare pool, Etang de La Bonde, windsurfing.
Club de Planche à Voile de l'Etang de la Bonde
M.Claude Vigne
☎ *90.77.64.95*

THE SEA

Coastal or deep-sea cruising is also very tempting, and there are two options: one is to join a course at any of the several clubs based along the coast; the other is to charter a yacht for a day, a weekend or longer. Sailing craft available for hire are new or nearly-new and fully equipped for safety and comfort. For those who want to participate in the mysterious world of rigging and watches, this will prove an unforgettable experience. Accompanied by an experienced crew, this type of sailing is accessible to beginners, and you can choose between a cruise along the coast between the Camargue and Hyères; exploring amongst the pretty sea inlets or *calanques*; or setting off from Hyères to discover the islands of Porquerolles, Port-Cros and Le Levant.

HIRE OF SAILING CRAFT AND WINDSURFERS ALONG THE COAST:

VAR
Hyères
Number of permanent/temporary moorings:
Port de l'Aygade 480/150
Port du Niel 127/2
La Capte 125/18
Hyères 1350/120

A SUN ODYSSEY YACHT

The World Windsurfing Championships are held here annually at the end of February at the Almanarre beach, by the Golfe de Giens.

Sailing and Windsurfing courses:
Mistral Center
Presqu'île de Giens
83400 Hyères
☎ *94.58.26.87*
Hyères Windsurf
Plage de l'Almanarre
☎ *94.38.51.62*
Base Nautique
Port-St-Pierre
83400 Hyères
☎ *94.38.88.67*

Hire of sailing craft:
Navigazur
Centre Commercial Nautisme
Le Port
83400 Hyères
☎ *94.57.26.09*

Hire of new or nearly-new boats:
Au Fil de l'Entrave
Centre Commercial Nautisme
14 avenue du Docteur Robin
83400 Hyères
☎ *94.57.33.13/94.57.61.69*
Galian Yachting Location
1846 route Almanarre
Hyères
☎ *94.38.63.77*
Pasquier Voile-Catamaran
Port Gavine
83400 Hyères
☎ *94.38.50.80*

Centre Nautisme
27 avenue du Docteur Robin
83400 Hyères
☎ *94.38.43.01*

Toulon
Number of permanent/temporary moorings: 1300/according to departures.

Courses:
Association Mistral Cassiopée
1 rue Hoche
83000 Toulon
☎ *94.62.12.12./94.62.12.62*
Club Nautique Le Pradet-La Garonne
B.P. Mairie Annexe
93220 Le Pradet
☎ *94.75.19.03*
Keelboard craft, windsurfers, surfing sailing and cruising.
Gerard Genta
Bateau Le Sicilien
83400 Porquerolles
☎ *94.58.30.61*
Tuna fishing, tuna-boat sea cruising, by the day or week, individuals or groups.
Yacht Club de Toulon
Plage du Mourillon
4eme Anse
Base Nautique
83000 Toulon
☎ *94.46.63.18*
Keelboard craft, windsurfing, catamaran.

Boat rental:
Quo Vadis Yachting
quai du Petit Rang
83000 Toulon
☎ *94.31.56.13/94.41.32.84*

Sailing and power boats, 6-15 metres, with or without skipper.

Accastillage Diffusion
15 quai du Petit Rang
83000 Toulon
☎ *94.41.30.10*
Hire of the full "Jeanneau" range.

Bandol
Number of permanent/temporary moorings: 1350/47

Hire:
Bandol-Bateau
10 boulevard Victor Hugo
Bandol
☎ *94.29.48.94*
Loca-Nautic
28 rue Pons
Bandol
☎ *94.32.42.47*
Astro Voile
allée Vivien
Bandol
☎ *94.32.23.30*
Locasail
Villa Antarès
Corniche Bonaparte
☎ *94.29.59.83*

BOUCHES-DU-RHONE

La Ciotat
Number of permanent/temporary moorings: 640/20

Société des Régates de La Ciotat
Nouveau Port de Plaisance
avenue Wilson
13600 La Ciotat
☎ *42.08.50.28*
Courses at various levels - keelboard craft, coastal and deep-sea cruising,

windsurfing, one week or longer; weekend cruising available in First Class (8 metres) craft.

Yachting Club Ciotaden
Port de Plaisance
13600 La Ciotat
☎ *42.08.50.28*
Facilities as above, plus accommodation available in studio apartment (sleeps 4) or half-pension in two-star hotel.

Société Nautique
Port de Plaisance
13600 La Ciotat
☎ *42.71.67.82*
Instruction in keelboard craft, catamaran, windsurfing, one or two weeks, half or full days. Motor-boat hire (no hire of sailing craft).

Polo Marine
Port de Plaisance
13600 La Ciotat
☎ *42.08.90.70*
Power boats for water-skiing and fishing.

Acqua Sun Boat
18, avenue F. Gassion
13600 La Ciotat
☎ *42.08.36.95*
Nautimer
3 bd. Anatole France
13600 La Ciotat
☎ *42.08.68.14*

Cassis
Number of permanent/temporary moorings: 450/23
Centre Culturel, Section Planche à Voile
9 place Montmorin
13260 Cassis
☎ *42.01.77.73 (off season)*
☎ *42.01.80.01 (in season)*
Instruction courses of 3/4/7 days or longer, and hire for 1 hour to 1 week or longer from May onwards.

VIEUX PORT, MARSEILLE

CALANQUES, MARSEILLE

Office de Tourisme
Place Baragnon
13260 Cassis
☎ *42.01.71.17*
Half- or full-day outings in a Delph 38 (10 metres) with skipper. No centre-board craft in Cassis.

Marseille
Number of permanent/temporary moorings:
L'Estaque 1450/50
Vieux Port 3200/40
Pointe Rouge 1200/10
Le Frioul 750/150

Courses :
Société Nautique Estaque Mourepiane
Promenade la Plage l'Estaque
13016 Marseille
☎ *91.46.01.40*
Sailing.
Pacific Palisades
Wind Park Port de la Pointe Rouge
13008 Marseille
☎ *91.73.54.37*
Sailing and windsurfing.
Yachting Club de la Pointe Rouge
Port de la Pointe Rouge
13008 Marseille
☎ *91.73.06.75*
Sailing and windsurfing.
Michel Astruc
25 avenue Reine Jeanne
13001 Marseille
Iles du Frioul
☎ *91.59.05.12*
Mini-cruising, fishing.

Hire:
Business Tourisme Loisirs
11 Traverse du Levant

13007 Marseille
☎ *91.31.16.87*
Climat International
96 Quai du Port
13002 Marseille
☎ *91.91.86.77*
Compagnie Mediterranéenne des Armateurs Gerants
1 quai Protis
13002 Marseille
☎ *91.56.15.59*
E.G.T.I.
20 quai Lazaret
13002 Marseille
☎ *91.90.61.03*

Carry-le-Rouet
Number of permanent/temporary moorings: 500/10

Courses:
Club de Carry-le-Rouet
☎ *42.45.09.21*

Martigues (Port de Carro)
Number of permanent/temporary moorings: 200/20

Courses:
Cercle de la Voile de Martigues
Base de Tholon
Quartier Touret de Vallier
13500 Martigues
☎ *42.80.12.94*
Sailing, windsurfing, cruising.

Boat rental:
Croisières Bleues
avenue Moulins de France
13500 Martigues
☎ *42.80.51.48*

Istres
Three stretches of water - Berre, l'Olivier
and Entressen.

Courses:
Association Nautique Omnisport Istréenne
Istrium du Sport
13800 Istres
☎ *42.56.21.33*
Sailing and windsurfing on the Etang de
Berre.
Centre Educatif et Culturel "Les Heures
Claires"
13800 Istres
☎ *42.56.34.39*
Sailing and windsurfing instruction with
loan of windsurfer in summer.
L'Apeli Base Nautique d'Entressen
13118 Entressen
☎ *90.50.52.39*
Sailing, windsurfing, Mediterranean
cruising.
Base nautique de l'Olivier
Quartier des Arnavaux
13800 Istres
☎ *42.55.51.52*
Windsurfer loan.

Fos-sur-Mer (Port de St-Gervais)
Number of permanent/temporary
moorings: 602/35

Courses:
Club de Voile
avenue des Palmiers
Mairie (Maison de la Mer)
13270 Fos-sur-Mer
☎ *42.05.34.51*
Centre Fosséen de Voile
Plage la Marinède
13270 Fos-sur-Mer
☎ *42.05.32.90/42.05.26.04*

CANAL AND RIVER CRUISING

For those who prefer the quiet life, an
alternative is river tourism; discover for
yourself the Rhône-Sète canal on a house
boat, from Beaucaire to Sète; or join a half-

CANAL CRUISING

or full-day expedition on a boat in the 'Little
Camargue', or on the Rhône, from Aigues-
Mortes up to Avignon. There are also firms
offering hire on cruising barges.

**Hire of boats on the Rhône to Sète
canal:**
⓯ Blue Line Camargue
quai du Canal
30200 St-Gilles
☎ *66.87.22.66*
⓰ Locaboat Plaisance
Port de Plaisance
30220 Aigues-Mortes
☎ *66.53.91.04*
⓱ Caminav
Base Fluviale
34130 Carnon
☎ *67.68.01.90*

**Outings and cruises on the Rhône-
Sète Canal:**
⓲ Yacht "Le Cygne"
Gerard Couly
15 rue Circulaire
30300 Beaucaire
☎ *66.59.35.62/66.59.45.08*
Half- or full-day trips on the Rhône,
departing from Lyon, Avignon, Arles or
Aigues-Mortes
⓳ L.P.M.
38 rue St-Jacques
13006 Marseille
☎ *91.53.57.47*
Hotel-barge 'Amerique' with seating for 70,
Beaucaire, Sète and the Rhône-Sète;
Etang de Thau, 6-day cruises. All year,
groups only.
⓳ Le Mireio
Office Municipal de Tourisme
☎ *95.25.61.33*
Route: Avignon - Villeneuve, 'The cruise of
the Kingdom'
⓰ Barge 'La Pescalune'
B.P. 76
30220 Aigues-Mortes
☎ *66.53.79.47*
Exploring the 'Petite Camargue', half- or
full-day trips.

WHITE-WATER SPORTS

French rivers lend themselves to all forms
of white-water sports, canoeing and
kayaking, rafting, hydrospeed and
canyoning.

Canoeing and Kayaking
Canoeing and kayaking are the oldest of
these. Originating from Canada, the
canoeist kneels down with a single paddle,
whereas in the kayak, of Eskimo origin, he
has a double paddle and is propelled from
the seated position. Canoeing and
kayaking are practised in more than 600
clubs with competitions at championship
and Olympic level. The French Federation
of Canoeing and Kayaking, the F.F.C.K.,
covers both sports and has in some of its
riverside or coastal centres set up a French

RAFTING IN UBAYE

School of Canoeing and Kayaking which aims more modestly at tourists and holiday-makers. The F.F.C.K. publishes maps and practical guides, including an annual guide to canoeing and kayaking holidays.

Rafting
Rafting is the leading white-water sport: a logical success because it's accessible to anyone without previous experience (the instructor looking after everything) and gives unforgettable thrills. Rafting is a team sport, a kind of river rodeo on a super-inflatable small boat armed with large inflated fenders.

Usually for four, six or ten, it is less frequently crewed by sixteen, only possible on the wider Canadian rivers in flood. According to type, rafting is done with either a single or double oar which is used by an experienced guide positioned in the middle of the boat, or supplemented by team members with single paddles. Less well-known is the "Hot Dog", an open inflatable kayak where one, two or three crew sit with single paddles.

Great thrills are guaranteed. Rafting is practised when the snow melts from the beginning of April to the end of September. Commercial firms offer from a one- to two-hour descent to half-day or full-day trips, often combined with hydrospeed and a hot meal, a barbecue on arrival. Protective clothing, windsurfing suit, helmet and lifejacket are provided. All you need is an old pair of trainers and some dry clothes to put on at the end of the trip!

Hydrospeed
For some daredevils, a large raft between the fast-flowing water and themselves is still too much. Wearing a helmet, wetsuit and hand protection they hurl themselves headfirst into the torrent clinging to a kind of water toboggan, the Hydrospeed. This sport is even more physical and aquatic than rafting.

Canyoning
Canyoning is a mixture of walking, swimming, inflatable boating, climbing and rappels: an adventurous mingling of the intoxication and dangers of them all. Find out about the weather before setting off for storms upstream when the snow melts can cause flash floods.

Choose a canyon appropriate to your ability and preferably make a one-day journey at the most, leaving early in the morning. If you consider that your basic techniques are inadequate, specialist services are available in most mountainous regions with canyons for caving and high-mountain guides are also experienced in this field.

Regional and national canoeing, kayaking and hydrospeed competitions are organized each year. Information from the Association des Sports d'Eaux Vives, Eric Olive, Conseil Général, B.P. 216, 04003 Digne-les-Bains ☎ 92.32.25.32. This association can send you information about the departmental organisations for white-water sports.

In Provence many associations or clubs, (commercial firms for rafting), offer courses and holidays for beginners and river descents in canyons for the more experienced.

RIVER UBAYE
The Ubaye is one of the most popular rivers of the *département* Alpes-de-Haute-Provence.

Canoeing and kayaking:
Introductions on a small stretch of water at Barcelonnette.
⑳ FFCK Alpes-de-Haute-Provence
Ecole Régionale du Canoë-Kayak et Sports d'Eau Vive
☎ *92.45.25.19*
Base de Loisirs d'Eygliers
05600 Eygliers
☎ *92.81.04.02*
Plan d'eau de Bachelard
04400 Barcelonnette (in season)

River descents with the Association Découverte
㉑ Base Eau Vive
Pont du Martinet
04340 Le Lauzet-sur-Ubaye
☎ *92.85.53.99*
Maison du Canoë-Kayak
2 rue Noël Ballay
75020 Paris
☎ *(1) 43.72.16.97*

Rafting and hydrospeed:
The Ubaye is an ideal spot for rafting and hydrospeed too:
㉑ AN Rafting Ubaye Aventure
☎ *92.85.54.90 (in summer)* ☎ *92.81.90.05 (out of season)*
AN Rafting is a large commercial firm with close links with F.F.C.K.

㉑ La Fresquière
04340 Le Lauzet-sur-Ubaye
㉒ AN Rafting Centre
15 rue Aufray
92110 Clichy
☎ *(1) 47.37.08.77*

Descents on the Martinet from Le Lauzet and from Barcelonnette to Le Lauzet:
㉓ France Raft
04850 Jausiers
☎ *92.84.60.17*
A subsidiary of a well-established firm in Switzerland, its bases are mainly on the rivers of the Alpes-du-Sud.

Canyoning:
㉔ Fun Adventure
La Bergerie
Le Martinet
04340 Meolan Revel
☎ *92.85.54.77*
Trips organized by the Bureau des Guides de l'Ubaye. Headquarters at the Barcelonnette Tourist Office.
☎ *92.81.04.07*

RIVER VERDON
The Verdon is the best-known river for canoeing.

Canoeing and kayaking:
㉕ Centre Plein Air Nature
Château de la Lagne
04120 Castellane
☎ *92.83.61.13*
Also offers canyoning.

Club de Canoë-kayak de Castellane
18, rue Nationale
04120 Castellane
☎ *92.83.70.61*
㉖ La Cadeno
La Mairie
04360 Moustiers-Sainte-Marie
☎ *92.74.68.40*

Rafting:
Verdon Animation Nature
La Palud-sur-Verdon
04120 Castellane
☎ *92.74.66.94 or 92.77.38.59 or 42.57.15.99*
㉕ AN Rafting
04120 Castellane
☎ *92.83.70.83*
㉖ Plein Air Nature
42 boulevard Victor Hugo
04000 Digne
☎ *92.31.51.09*

Canyoning:
㉕ Verdon Animation Nature
La-Palud-sur-Verdon
04120 Castellane
☎ *92.74.66.94 or 92.77.38.59 or 42.57.15.99*
㉕ Centre Plein Air Nature
Château de La Lagne
04120 Castellane
☎ *92.83.61.13*

RIVER DURANCE
Canoeing and Kayaking:
㉗ Club de Canoë-Kayak de Sisteron
(Alain Toureille) 24 avenue du Jabron
04200 Sisteron
☎ *92.61.34.18*

RIVER RHONE
Canoeing and Kayaking:
㉘ Trinquetaille Sailing Club
(M.Comte) 4 quai Saint-Pierre
13200 Arles
☎ *90.93.11.60*
㉙ Office du Tourisme de Cassis
place Baragnon
☎ *42.01.71.17*
Sea-going kayaks can be hired; a swimming certificate for at least 50 yards is required.
㉙ Club de Canoë-kayak de Cassis
avenue de la Viguerie
☎ *42.01.18.58*
Organizes water expeditions to the most beautiful places in the area.

Descending the Sorgue from Fontaine-de-Vaucluse to Isle-sur-Sorgue:
㉚ Kayak Vert
Michel Melani
84800 Fontaine-de-Vaucluse
☎ *90.20.35.44*

Courses for groups and individuals:
Club de Canoë-kayak Islois
La Cigalette
Isle-sur-Sorgue
☎ *90.38.33.22 or 90.20.64.70*

RIDING AND BIKING

HOLIDAYS ON THE TRAIL

HORSE RIDING

Modern transport will have brought you to the Provençal countryside or the mountains between the Rhône and the Durance, but why not exchange your car for a horse at one of the riding establishments mentioned in this guide?

Many centres accept holidaymakers who are passing through and just wish to have an hour's ride, a *promenade*, accompanied or not. You could also go out for a half-day trek, while perhaps the most pleasant excursions are full-day trips with a break for a picnic lunch, your own supply brought with you in the saddle bag.

The French Tourist organization has ensured that riders wishing to have holidays with horses are well catered for. Types of holiday which are offered vary from the very popular *Weekend de Randonnée* when riders are away from the base for one night, to the *Grande Randonnée* which lasts five days or more and which is aimed at more experienced riders.

Accompanied treks include the price of the guide and you will be taken as a group. As tours usually consist of loops there is no need to retrace the route or return to the centre at night. Such trips enable you to meet the local people and appreciate the landscape and history of the places you visit in an ideal and leisurely manner.

Reservations can be made to suit age requirements and some centres specialize in holidays for young riders, paying careful attention to individual ability.

For those with advanced riding ability it is possible to go out alone (or as a private group of friends) on itineraries with overnight stays, meals etc organized by the centre. Most establishments offer special rates, particularly out of season, for groups of six to eight riders and it is sometimes possible to arrange special '*à la carte*' treks outside scheduled itineraries. Reservations should be made as far in advance as possible. You should state your age, riding ability, weight and your exact requirements. A deposit equivalent to 30% is usually required. Before leaving the centre you should ensure that you know what you have paid for, such as board and lodging and baths, etc. You may need to hire a tent. If an animal is deemed to have been over-worked or any tack is lost or damaged the cost will be deducted from your deposit.

Accommodation offered on equestrian holidays is often in modest *dortoirs* (dormitories) or in *gîtes d'étape* but there are also trips which lay emphasis on enjoying the gastronomic delights of the region at the end of each day !

Where riding centres are located in or close to the towns in the gazetteer section of this guide they have been included but in addition there is an excellent booklet published by the Direction Nationale pour le Tourisme Equestre and any would-be riders in France would do well to obtain a copy. It gives a contact address for each département in France and hundreds of names and addresses of regional centres (address on page 19).

Other useful addresses:
Association Régionale de Tourisme Equestre de Provence (ATEP)
(*départements* 04,05,13,84)
"L'homme à cheval",
13810 Eygalières
☎ 90.95.90.57

HORSE RIDING, VERDON

Association Départementale de Tourisme
Equestre, Alpes-de-Haute-Provence
M.G. Hernandez
4 rue des Charrois
04000 Digne
☎ 92.31.18.83
Ferme Equestre la Fenière
quartier Champarlaud
04200 Peipin
☎ 92.62.44.02/92.62.41.95
Courses and holidays at the farm with
accommodation in a *gîte*; camping
expeditions and staying in *gîtes* (Lure
mountains, Digne pre-alps)

The following riding centres offer outings
and expeditions in the region:

Alpes-de-Haute-Provence
❶ Centre Equestre de Terre-Neuve
04400 St-Pons
Barcelonnette
☎ 92.81.25.78
❷ Plein Air Nature
B.P. 129
04000 Digne
❸ Association Départementale de
Tourisme Equestre
42 boulevard Victor Hugo
04000 Digne
☎ 92.31.07.01
❸ Les Cavaliers du Verdon
04360 Moustiers-Ste-Marie
☎ 92.74.60.10
❹ Ranch les Pionniers
04120 La Palud-sur-Verdon
☎ 92.77.38.30
❺ Centre Equestre Château Laval
route de Valensole

04800 Gréoux-les-Bains
☎ 92.78.08.16

Bouches-du-Rhône
❻ Association Départementale du
Tourisme Equestre
Mas de Bouquet
Chemin d'Auriol
13790 Peynier
☎ 42.53.00.32

RIDING IN THE LUBERON

❼ Association la Provence à Cheval
quartier St-Joseph,
13950 Cadolive
☎ 42.04.66.76
Outdoor riding on horses and ponies for beginners. For those with some experience, outings, expeditions lasting from two to seven days:
Garlaban, Ste-Baume, Ste-Victoire, Alpes-de-Haute-Provence, *gîte* accommodation for individuals and groups.
❻ Centre Equestre du Haut de l'Arc
Mas de Bouquet
chemin d'Auriol
13790 Peynier
☎ 42.53.00.32

MOUNTAIN-BIKING

This is an activity full of vitality and a marvellous means of escape, discovery and access to nature.
The mountain-bike was first developed in the United States towards the end of the 70s and, since 1983, France as the European mountain-biking paradise, has seen a particular growth in the sport's popularity.
In general, mountain-bike routes are marked on existing walking and riding routes an departmental maps but nonetheless they have their own identity and are varied according to different levels

MOUNTAIN-BIKING

Vaucluse
❽ Comité Départementale du Tourisme Equestre du Vaucluse
28 place Roger Salengro
84300 Cavaillon
☎ 90.78.04.49
❾ Cercle Hippique du Buis
Mas du Buis Joucas
84220 Gordes
☎ 90.05.78.26
Outings, weekend expeditions, holidays and courses.
❿ Le Mas de Recaute
84360 Lauris
☎ 90.08.29.58
Excursions, 2-week treks, accommodation in *gîtes d'étape* with accompanying vehicle: Lubéron, Provençal Colorado, Hautes-Alpes, Devoluy, the Cévennes, Verdon. Accommodation in *gîtes*.
⓫ Cheval Nomade
Col du Pointu
84480 Bonnieux
☎ 90.04.72.01
Accompanied treks under the leadership of two specialists in long expeditions in Haute-Provence and the Camargue.
The organization allows a choice of accommodation: comfortable 2 or 3 star hotels or, closer to nature, at inns or under canvas.

of difficulty. These take into account elements such as severe gradients, the nature of the terrain sand, mud, etc and technically difficult stretches. They rarely follow tarmac roads and prefer forest routes, farm and mule tracks and the transhumance trails followed by migrating flocks.
Each circuit is numbered and marked on a waymark, with a pictogram distinct from the other waymark symbols used so as to avoid any confusion (two circles joined to a triangle) and is colour-coded corresponding to the degree of difficulty: green (very easy), blue (easy), red (difficult) and black (very difficult); exactly the same as for ski pistes.
Pocket maps which are easy to carry with you (9cm x 11cm in size) show the VTT/FFC (French Cycling Federation) information points, enabling you to visualize the outline of existing routes, appreciate their difficulty and length and acquire the necessary practical information for a good expedition. Information is available through public information offices, Town Halls, Tourist Offices, Information Bureaux and in specialist shops, mountain-bike and bike-hire centres.
Mountain-biking can, of course, be done

MOUNTAIN-BIKING

by the individual alone either with his own equipment or by hiring it from one of the many centres available. Careful preparation for your excursion is recommended and some hirers can suggest suitable routes. If you wish, and have the time, write to the mountain-bike centres or the *gîtes d'étape* which often combine this activity with walking or other open-air sporting activities. There are routes for all abilities ranging form half-day expeditions to a weekend or, at the most, five days in a small group with a maximum of 12 people of the same level.

In Provence, you can follow the route of film locations used as the setting for Marcel Pagnol's work *Jean de Florette* and *Manon des Sources*; you will discover villages with old streets, little country roads in Lubéron, or the beauty of Mont Ventoux, the Dentelles de Montmirail or the Baronnies. Mountain-biking is not simply a means of transport demanding physical effort alone. It is primarily a way of exploring the physical, cultural and historic areas of a region.

Alpes-de-Haute-Provence
V.T.T. Rando 04
19 chemin du Tivoli
04000 Digne-les-Bains
☎ 92.31.62.90
Rando 04 is without doubt the departmental organization most interested in mountain-biking. It promotes this activity within the *département*, draws up maps of the best routes and offers various introductory courses to mountain-biking. A list of the mountain-biking clubs in the *département* is also available from them.
Centre National de V.T.T.
04660 Chamtercier
☎ 92.31.34.02

Hiring of mountain-bikes:
In Digne
Gallardo ☎ 92.31.05.29 and Sports 2000, boulevard Gassendi ☎ 92.31.51.40
In Manosque
Alpes-Provence-Aventure
Cirem-Z.I.,St-Joseph, 04100 Manosque
☎ 92.87.48.44 or 92.72.65.77

Vaucluse
Martine Tempier "Les Routes du Lubéron" route de Lacoste, 84560 Menerbes
☎ 90.72.37.45
Discover Lubéron by bike or mountain-bike. Theme days: "On Manon's routes" in the wake of Marcel Pagnol's films; and "Wheels of Lubéron".

Transhumance
B.P.9, 84004 Avignon ☎ 90.95.57.81
Introduction to mountain-biking, day expeditions and courses. Long-distance mountain-biking over several days, tourist cycling expeditions in the Dentelles de Montmirail, the mountains of Vaucluse and the Lubéron regional park.
Detroit
Eric Neuville, angle rue Trogue Pompée, Baffavon, 84110 Vaison
☎ 90.36.03.57
Guided expeditions in groups on request into the Dentelles de Montmirail, the Ventoux, the Baronnies. Mountain-bikes for hire.

Gard
Maison des Terres de Sommières
route d'Uzès, 30250 Sommières
☎ 66.77.75.37 or 66.77.70.39
Mountain-bike hire, circuits waymarked on the Terres de Sommières.
Nature et Loisirs
Mas de la Garonne, 30700 St-Maximin
☎ 66.22.79.40

GOLF

TEE OFF IN PROVENCE

Golf was first played in the Pyreneees, on the Basque coast and in Brittany, all places which, over the past hundred years, have been the favoured holiday and retirement retreats of wealthy English families. Anecdote has it that the first golf course in France was 'designed' by two Scots officers from Wellington's army when they were quartered in Pau in 1814 during the Peninsula War. What is certain is that the first golf club in France was opened at Pau in 1856 and that its membership was still almost exclusively British until the 1930s! The course at Dinard in Brittany was founded in 1887 to meet the needs of British residents, with the course at Biarritz a fashionable resort of royalty and high society created a year later and that at Compiègne in Picardy seven years after that.

The game was, however, played only by a small minority and developed very slowly in France compared with its neighbours Spain and Portugal where foreign vistitors enjoyed much better facilities. It was not until the 1980s, following the fashion for tennis, that interest in the game of golf began to flourish. Ten years ago, French golf clubs boasted 43,000 members but this figure had trebled by 1987, divided equally between men and women. Nine and 18-hole courses were designed, often as an integral part of a sports complex, and there are today more than 200 clubs with the number rising annually.

In Provence, golf courses are often laid out on *domaines* or private estates or around a traditional *mas* or farmhouse; situated amidst oak or pine woods, olive groves and vineyards. Here players can enjoy the magnificent scenery of mountain landscape or Mediterranean Sea.

Most courses are private though non-members and non-playing spectators are made welcome.

Experienced players should present their handicap certificate as regular competitions are held at weekends, and beginners may be required to pass a test of competence before playing. Green fees vary though in general are more expensive than in Britain and are usually quoted by the day rather than by the round. In high season it is advisable to reserve a tee at least two days in advance and especially at weekends. Most courses will close on Tuesdays.

Listed below are the principal 18-hole courses in Provence. Note that the recommended hotels can help organize tuition courses if required and may also offer all-in prices for accommodation and green fees.

❶ Aix-en-Provence
Golf d'Aix Marseille
Domaine de Riquetti
13290 Les Milles
☎ 42.24.20.41
6 km from Aix-en-Provence off the Aix-Marseille autoroute exiting at Les Milles, then the D9 towards Marignane. The course is on the left after 4 km.
Flat, tree-lined 18-hole par 72 course. Min handicap 36. Green fees: weekdays 220FF, weekends 400FF. Coaching available, courses Jul-Aug. Bar and restaurant.

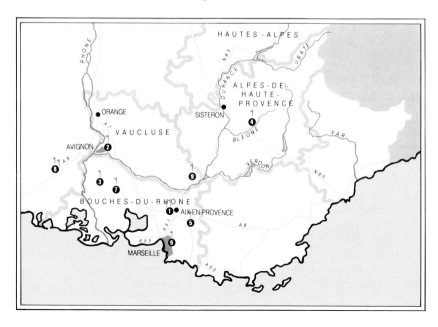

Hotels
Hôtel Pullman le Roi René ***
Aix-en-Provence
☎ 42.37.61.00.
Novotel Beaumanoir ***
Aix-en-Provence
☎ 42.27.47.50
Hôtel Paul Cézanne ***
Aix-en-Provence
☎ 42.26.43.73

❶ Aix-en-Provence
Golf de Cabriès Calas
Domaine du Boulard
13480 Cabriès
From Aix take the Marseille-Aix autoroute, exiting at Plan de Campagne (Aix-ouest), then RD9.
Technically difficult 18-hole par 72 course with water hazards and undulating woodland. No handicap requirement. Green fees: weekdays 130FF, weekends 150FF. Coaching available. Bar and restaurant.

❷ Avignon
Golf Club de Châteaublanc
route de Châteaublanc
84310 Morières-les-Avignon
☎ 90.33.39.08
From Avignon follow the RN7 towards Salon-de-Provence or the A7 exiting at Avignon Sud towards Avignon and then towards the aerodrome.
Long 18-hole par 72 course with artificial lakes and small greens. There is an additional 9-hole, par 28 course. Min handicap 35. Green fees: weekdays 160FF, weekends 250FF. Coaching available. Bar and restaurant.

Hotels
Le Paradou ***
Morières-les-Avignon
☎ 90.33.34.15
Le Mercure ***
route de Marseille
Avignon Sud
☎ 90.88.91.10
La Garlande *
Avignon
☎ 90.85.08.85

❸ Les Baux-de-Provence
Golf des Baux-de-Provence
Domaine de Manville
13520 Les Baux-de-Provence
☎ 90.54.37.02
From Marseille take the A7 exiting at Avignon Sud for St-Rémy and Maussane; or take the Salon-de-Provence exit in the direction of Arles, Mouriès and Maussane.
Situated in delightful Provençal countryside with views of the Alpilles massif, there are two 9-hole courses here, par 27 and par 36. Min handicap requirement 35. Green fees: weekdays 150FF, weekends 200FF.
Hotels
Le Mas d'Aigret ***
Baux
☎ 90.54.33.54
Le Prés de Baux ***
Maussane
☎ 90.54.40.40.
Le Val Baussenc ***
Maussane
☎ 90.54.38.90

❹ Digne-les-Bains
Golf de Digne-les-Bains
St-Pierre-de-Gaubert

GOLF IN PROVENCE

04000 Digne
☎ 92.32.38.38
6 km south of Digne.
Recently constructed 18-hole par 73
course with artificial lakes and tree
plantations. Min handicap 35. Green fees:
140-220FF according to season. Coaching
available. Bar and restaurant.
Hotels
L'Ermitage Napoleon ***
Digne
☎ 92.31.01.09
L'Hôtel du Grand Paris ***
Digne
☎ 92.31.11.15
Hôtel du Golf (on site) **
☎ 92.31.30.90
Tonic Hôtel **
Vallon des Eaux Chaudes
☎ 40.19.04.05

❺ Fuveau
Golf International de Château l'Arc
Domaine de Château l'Arc
13710 Fuveau
☎ 42.53.28.38
*From Aix take the A7 in the direction of
Nice exiting at Le Canet towards Toulon,
Trets and Labargue, then the du Rousset
industrial zone, Trets and the allée de
Château l'Arc. The golf course is
signposted.*
Technically demanding 18-hole par 72
course with the largest green in Europe -
over 2,500 square metres - numerous
bunkers and water hazards. Handicap
requirements: weekends 28 (ladies), 24
(men). Green fees: 230-330FF. Coaching
available. Bar and restaurant.

Hotels
Le Mas de la Bertrande ***
Beaurecueil
☎ 42.66.90.09
Novotel Beaumanoir ***
Aix-en-Provence
☎ 42.27.47.50
Relais Ste-Victoire ***
Beaurecueil
☎ 42.28.94.98

❻ Marseille
Golf Country Club La Salette
Impasse des Vaudrans
13011 Marseille
☎ 91.27.12.16
*From Marseille take the A50 in the
direction of Aubagne, exiting at La
Valentine.*
This is a technically demanding 18-hole,
par 70 course, with an additional 9-hole,
par 27 course. The undulating layout
presents interesting hazards such as dry
stone walls and water obstacles and
boasts marvellous sea views. Min
handicap 35. Green fees: 180-250FF.
Coaching available. Bar and restaurant.
Hotel
Novotel ***
St-Menet
☎ 91.43.90.60

❼ Mouriès
Golf Club de Servanes
Domaine de Servanes
13890 Mouriès
☎ 90.47.59.95
*35 km from Avignon take A7 exiting at
Cavaillon Nord towards St-Rémy,*

*Massagne and Mouriès; or the RN133
Salon-de-Provence exit, then D5 towards
Mouriès.*
Set amidst the Alpilles massif, this 18-hole,
par 72 course features tall trees and lakes
with three greens set on islands. Min
handicap 35. Green fees: weekdays
180FF, weekends 250FF. Coaching
available. Bar and restaurant .
Hotel
Hôtel de Servanes (on site) **
☎ 90.47.50.03

❶ Nîmes
Golf de Nîmes Campagne
Route de St-Gilles
30000 Nîmes
☎ 66.70.17.37
*From Nîmes in the direction of St-Gilles on
the D42 then follow the chemin du Mas de
Campagne, 8 km from Nîmes.*
Very attractive wooded 18-hole, par 72
course, though the water hazards require
some technical expertise. Min handicap 32
weekdays, 28 (ladies) and 24 (men) at
weekends. Green fees: weekdays 200FF,
weekends 250-350 FF.
Hotel
Hôtel les Aubruns ****
☎ 66.70.10.44

❶ Nîmes
Golf des Hauts de Nîmes
Vacquerolles

30900 Nîmes
☎ 66.23.33.33
*From Nîmes take the péripherique ouest in
the direction of Alès and then exit at Le
Vigan.*
Undulating 18-hole par 72 course with
difficult greens. No handicap requirement.
Green fees: weekdays 160FF, weekends
230FF. Bar and restaurant .
Hotels
Hôtel Imperator ****
Nîmes
☎ 66.21.90.30
Le Pré Gallofre ***
route de Generac
☎ 66.29.65.41

❶ Pierrevert
Golf de Pierrevert
Domaine de la Grande Motte
04860 Pierrevert
☎ 92.72.17.19
*From Manosque, take the D6 route de la
Bastide des Jourdans (15 km from
Pierrevert).*
Technically difficult undulating 18-hole, par
72. No handicap requirements. Green fees:
160-220FF. Bar and restaurant.
Hotels
Villa Borghèse ****
Gréoux-les-Bains
☎ 92.78.00.91
Le Mirvy Familial ****
☎ 90.77.83.23

MOTORING TOURS

This chapter suggests eight itineraries to help you explore Provence region by region. We have chosen minor roads where possible to make the journey more pleasant for drivers and less arduous for cyclists. These routes connect up the main historic sites and places of architectural, artistic and ecological interest. They also take you to many of the smaller towns and fascinating hilltop villages typical of this part of France, as well as to some of the seaside resorts along the Mediterranean coastline.

For each itinerary we have indicated a number of 'staging posts': towns where you will find good restaurants and hotel accommodation. Most of these, together with the main features for which they are noted, are listed in the Gazetteer section.

Ranging from 110 to 292 km in length, these drives can be varied to suit individual taste. You can go at your own speed, making a rapid tour with just a glance at some of the places of interest, or spend several leisurely days, stopping as you please, and deviating from the suggested route if you feel like it.

The maps (scale 1:250,000) show the places of special interest in each area, and the starting point of each drive is cross-referenced to the atlas at the back of the book, enabling you to plan itineraries of your own.

THE RHONE DELTA AND THE CAMARGUE

180 km
Map ref
135 C4

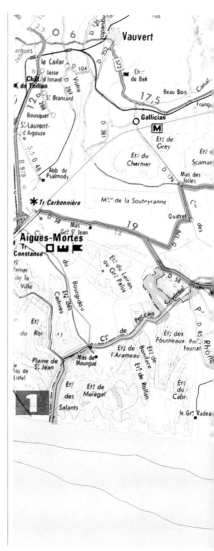

Starting from Arles this tour runs through the flat rice fields and salt marshes of the Camargue and its Regional Nature Park, with its wide horizons and famous herds of bulls and wild white horses. Other recommended staging posts are Aigues-Mortes and Les Saintes-Maries-de-la-Mer. **Arles**, departure point for this tour, retains its unfailing reputation as a lively centre for a wide range of cultural and other activities: bullfighting; folklore festivals in true local style with Arlésiennes in costume and *gardians*, or cowherds, on horseback; or international photographic conventions with countless showings and exhibitions. At the heart of the old town, stretching along the Rhône under its carapace of brown-tiled roofs, relics of antiquity like the Roman arena and amphitheatre rub shoulders with such Romanesque masterpieces as the church of St-Trophime and its cloister. Nearby you can take a melancholy stroll among tombs in the green and shady Alyscamps cemetery, or visit the Arlaten museum created by the writer Mistral, an ethnographic collection reflecting the vital character of the town and Provence as a whole.

From Arles take the N572 across the head of the Camargue, between the Great Rhône and the Little Rhône and on into the Gard, to reach **St-Gilles**, worth the detour for the Romanesque façade of its church, superbly sculptured and reminiscent, in general style, of the façade of St-Trophime. Then the D179 and D58 run through a fairly wild landscape dotted with the marshes that have given the town of **Aigues-Mortes** (dead waters) its name. Founded by St-Louis in the 13th century, it was originally little more than a port overlooked by the Tower of Constance. Then a few inhabited suburbs were added, surrounded by a rampart. Extremely well preserved, the wall, now topped with a roadway and flanked by towers, is joined to the Tower of Constance by a 16th-century bridge. From the top of the tower, 40 metres high, the view stretches frdom the Cévennes to the Camargue. Turning back eastwards, the D58, winding between rice fields and farmhouses to the Sylvereal bridge, leads eventually to the **Parc Naturel Régional de Camargue**, a nature reserve where herds of the famous white horses and fighting bulls and great flocks of birds enliven the entire landscape.

Les Saintes-Maries-de-la-Mer on the D38 is best known for its twice-yearly gatherings of gypsies from all over Europe (in May and October). The town's Baroncelli Museum reflects the history, wildlife, dress and customs of the region. The main architectural feature is the Romanesque church, fortified during the period of Saracen and other pirate invasions. In its crypt is a richly dressed and bejewelled statue of Saint Sarah, patroness of gypsies, which is carried in procession

through the town to the seashore on 24 May each year. The upper chapel, decorated with painted 18th-century wood carvings, opens onto a balcony which overlooks the town, the sea and the countryside. The outstanding wildlife of the Camargue consists largely of an incredible variety of wading and water birds, both resident and migratory, which, with care and patience, you can study throughout the area. The Pont de Gau bird sanctuary, 5km along the D570, shows them in their natural habitat, and also has aviaries for species which cannot survive in the wild. The preservation of many of these birds was made possible by the creation of the Réserve National de Camargue and Réserve Départementale des Impériaux, in the middle of the Regional Nature Park, access to which is limited to a walkway on the sea wall strictly reserved for pedestrians and cyclists. An information centre at **Ginès** houses a permanent audio-visual exhibition of protected bird sanctuaries.

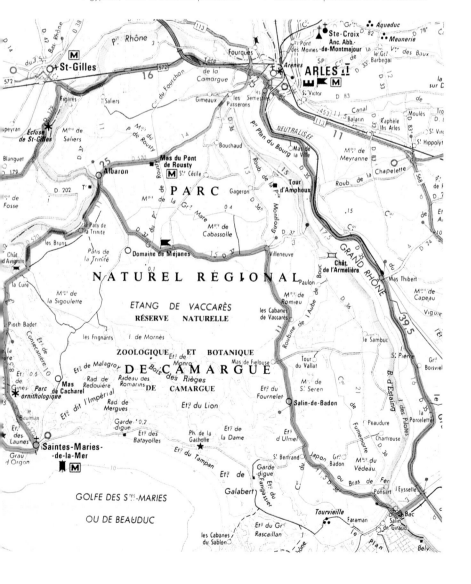

THE CAMARGUE

the bleak marshes. Surrounded by a park full of countless rare trees, this château in the classical style, with its terraced belvedere, boasts a round bell tower and is decorated with sculptures, chimneyed turrets and gargoyles. Still on the same road, the Musée Camarguais at the Mas du Pont de Rousty, traces the history of the Camargue from the Stone Age to the present day. Return as fas as Albaron, go right along the D37 to Villeneuve, and follow the D36c south to the Domaine de la Capelière where there is an Information Centre offering recommended walks through the village streets to take in several important exhibitions.

Following the D36a and then D36 past the salt mining village of **Salins de Giraud**, you drive along the edge of the strange and spectacular shimmering salt marshes. Farther on, from special observation posts in the Domaine de la Palissade, you can see herds of horses and cattle roaming free. To return to Arles, follow the road round the other side of Salins de Giraud, and take the D35 to bring you back to the opposite bank of the Rhône.

Continuing along the D570 you soon reach the remarkable 18th-century Château d'Avignon, a hothouse flower in the heart of

AVIGNON AND THE ALPILLES

157 km
Map ref
129 F5

A figure of eight tour with, as its starting point, Avignon, one of France's leading cities rich in museums and art collections as well as beautiful architecture. The drive includes an excursion into the rocky hill landscape of the Alpilles. The recommended staging posts are Les Baux-de-Provence, Fontvieille and Arles.

Crowning glory of Provences's artistic and cultural life from the 14th to 18th century, **Avignon** is still one of the most prestigious cities in the region. In summer it becomes the centre of French and indeed European theatrical life and offers throughout the year permanent feasts of historic art and architecture. In the place du Palais, dominated by the Romanesque cathedral of Notre-Dames-des-Doms, stands the immense Gothic conglomeration of the Palais des Papes, richly decorated with frescoes. At the foot of the square, the Petit Palais museum houses the important Campana collection of early Italian painting and masters of the Avignon school. And from the terraced garden of the Rocher des Doms views over the surrounding countryside include Villeneuve-lès-Avignon on the other side of the river, and stretching half way across, the famous St-Bénézet bridge, better known as the Pont d'Avignon.

Dominated by the Fort St-André perched on a rock above, Villeneuve-lès-Avignon was formerly a residence of the cardinals. Paintings in its municipal museum include the *Coronation of the Virgin* by Enguerrand Quarton. The Chartreuse du Val de Bénédiction has the tomb of Pope Innocent VI by Barthélemy Cavalier and, in the

chapel, frescoes by Matteo Giovanetti. Taking the N570 south from Avignon, follow the D28 along "La Montagnette"; a detour to the west along the D81 leads to the abbey of St-Michel-du-Frigolet set in a wooded valley carpeted with thyme. Only the church, cloisters and chapel, with wood carvings donated by Anne of Austria, formed the original monastery. The rest of the structure is a 19th-century Gothic revival. Ten km farther on you enter **Tarascon** by the Porte Condamine. Close to the pretty Cloître des Cordeliers is the Romanesque church of Ste-Marthe with paintings by Parrocel and de Mignard, and a tomb attributed to the school of Francesco Laurana. By the river stands the elegantly decorated Château du Roi René. Leave Tarascon by the D99, heading east towards **Les Alpilles**. Along this chalky range whose whiteness seems to enhance the strength of the sun, patches of more or less dense woodland cling, olive trees mingling with oak. On the plain below, **St-Rémy-de-Provence** comes into view, with plane trees shading the little streets that lead to the place Favier, where fine houses line the square. The Renaissance Hôtel Mistral de Mondragon, now the Musée des Alpilles, exhibits local art and folklore, and

the Hôtel de Sade houses remains excavated from the archaeological site at **Glanum**, 2 km south on the D5. Together with Les Antiques, Glanum ranks among the best-preserved examples from the Gallo-Roman period. A lane opposite Les Antiques leads to the former monastery of St-Paul-de-Mausole; now a hospice, it is where the painter Van Gogh stayed for a time. Following the line of Les Alpilles westwards, you pass a fine Renaissance house and the Cardinal's Tower, before veering off south on the D27 through the mountains and down by the Val d'Enfer "Hell's Valley" wedged between giant needles of rock to the village of **Les Baux-de-Provence**. Here the old houses and mansions of the 15th and 16th centuries, below the ruins of the great castle destroyed by Richelieu, are surprisingly uniform in style and are strongly evocative of the town's past splendour. On one side thorny brushwood clings to a jumble of rock, contrasting with narrow streets on the other where elegant Renaissance façades look down on the shining cobbles. The lively craftsmen's workshops seem to stand guard on the memories of this uninhabited village and its ruined château. Near the picturesque village of **Fontvieille**

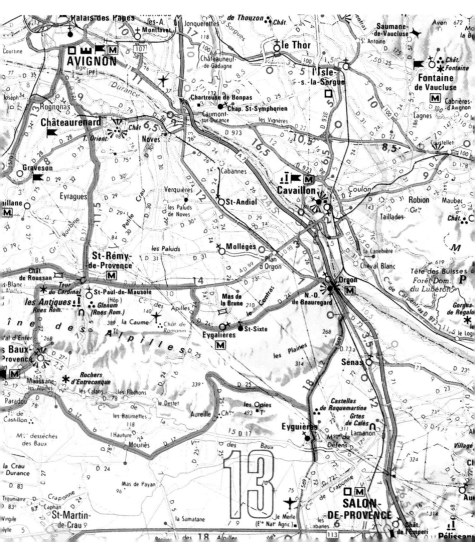

DAUDET'S MILL

reached by the D78f, then D17, are the
Château de Montauban, home of Alphonse
Daudet, and the Daudet museum set in the
windmill celebrated in his famous book
Lettres de mon Moulin.
The D17a passes close to the Hypogée du
Castellet, a prehistoric burial ground, and
leads on to the abbey of Montmajour, one
of the most beautiful Romanesque
buildings in Provence. From here take
either the N750 into Arles or D82 towards

the Alpilles. Just before **Maussane-les-
Alpilles** via the D78e, D78 and D17 are
olive groves, where the traditional oil
industry still thrives. Some 6km farther on
the road passes in front of the delightful
Renaissance manor of Mas de la Tour-du-
Brau, 500m before **Mouriès**, the leading
olive-growing commune in the whole of
France. Via the D17, D25a you pass
through **Aureille**, close to the Château de
Roquemartine, before reaching **Eyguières**
on the D569, where you will be lulled by
the sound of its many fountains including a
particularly lovely one known as the 'Coquille'.
The old town of **Orgon** via the D569 and
N7, has a fortified gate and pretty
Renaissance house near the church.
Castle ruins dominate the town, while
winding pathways to the chapel of Notre-
Dame-de-Beauregard culminate in a
magnificent view. Leaving by the D24b,
you reach the very pretty village of
Eygalières, rising by gentle stages from the
plain to the rock above. Its houses seem to
grow out of the rough stone finely shaped
by man's hand, eloquent expression of
Provence's characteristic affinity with
nature. Climb up past the church, the
grand'rue and the recreation ground for
views embracing the whole colourful
landscape of the Durance valley and
Alpilles chain.
From Eygalières, drive on towards St-
Rémy-de-Provence (D24 and D99) arriving
back in Avignon via the D571.

THE MONTAGNE DE LURE AND THE ROUTE NAPOLEON

133 km
Map ref
132 C2

Another shortish tour, this time in Haute-
Provence, running from Sisteron up and
over the Lure summit and down to the
Durance again. From here you branch off
to the spa town of Digne and back again by
way of the *Route Napoléon*, through alpine
pastures and lavender fields. Digne-les-
Bains is one of the recommended staging
posts along with Sisteron.
Four large towers greet you at the avenue
de Verdun entrance to the old town of
Sisteron. In the place Général-de-Gaulle
stands the cathedral of Notre-Dame-des-
Pommiers, Romanesque stongly influenced
by nearby Lombardy. Skirt around the
cathedral and down towards the clock
tower surmounted by a beautiful bell turret.
From there a network of narrow lanes and
passages with covered ways stretching as
far as the rues Mercerie, Droitte and
Saunerie, lead down to the Durance.
Perched on a rock is an imposing citadel, a
mixture of many different periods: a 13th-
century castle, a beautiful 15th-century
chapel in two colours of blonde sandstone
and grey limestone, 16th-century walls,
and an amazing 19th-century underground
stairway, hewn out of the rock.
Follow the D53 alongside the forest of
Jabron, which covers the northern flank of
the Lure ridge, then the D113 through a

series of hairpin bends to the summit with panoramic views of the valleys and mountains. Lower down, the 12th- and 13th-century abbey of Notre-Dame-de-Lure appears, set in a small valley amidst lime trees. From **St-Etienne-les-Orgues**, at the foot of the mountain, take the D951 eastward to **Cruis**, a charming village huddled around a monastery conspicuous for its stone-shingled roof and the glazed belfry of its church. Green woodland borders this whole stretch of road, with little streams tumbling down the mountainside and between the hills. The D951 and then the D101 lead us to St-Donat, once a lonely retreat of a hermit-priest to whom its early Romanesque church, standing on a grassy knoll, is dedicated. Descending gently towards the Durance you cross the N9, which passes close to the splendid priory of Ganagobie, 10 km to the south. The D4 takes you across the river; on the far bank the once fortified village of **Les Mées** continues in a curious line of rocks, the shapes, according to legend, of penitents turned to stone.

From Malijai follow the *Route Napoléon*, N85, taken by the Emperor on his return

THE PENITENTS AT MEES

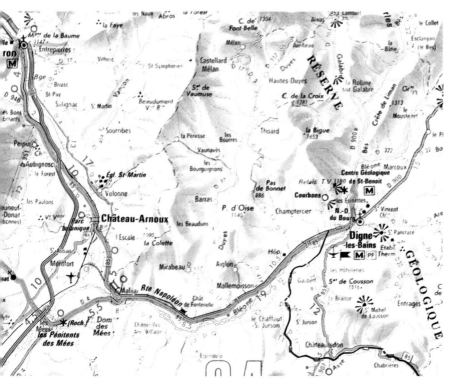

from Elba, to **Digne-les-Bains**, lavender-growing capital and gateway to the foothills of the Alps. After admiring the 14th- and 15th-century mural paintings and sculpture in the ancient Romanesque cathedral of Notre-Dame-du-Bourg, and the two-tone façade of the 15th-century cathedral of St-Jérome, carry on past the tower, the rue du Figuier, the Rochas slopes and the rue du Trou-du-Four, to reach the place Pied-de-Ville and old Gaubert gate. The Thiers and Gambetta boulevards lead on to the Alexandra David-Neel Foundation which houses a Tibetan cultural centre and numerous documents collected by this great Asian explorer. Also at Digne is the Information Centre of the 665-acre Haute-Provence Geological Nature Reserve. Finallly, you follow the *Route Napeoléon* back to Sisteron, passing through **Château-Arnoux**, a village with an early 16th-century château, combining late Gothic with early Renaissance, and crossing the Durance near **Volonne**, whose 17th-century château has a stairwell with superb plasterwork decoration.

HISTORIC TOWNS AND HILLTOP VILLAGES IN THE LUBERON

292 km
Map ref
136 A1

With Cavaillon as departure point, this tour meanders through the Lubéron mountains, a protected region of picturesque countryside and peaceful forests, of vineyards, olive groves and almond trees. Recommended staging posts are Bonnieux, Pertuis, Apt and Gordes.
Cavaillon, made famous for its melons by Alexandre Dumas is, with Châteaurenard, the most important market gardening centre in Provence, indeed all France. Its Roman arch, splendid synagogue and old town houses are noteworthy, while the cathedral of St-Véran is Romanesque with Gothic carvings and a Baroque interior. After leaving Cavaillon, little villages punctuate the small roads of the Lubéron. Built by a courageous peasant population inspired by a profound love of the land, they grew up little by little around newly dug wells drawing the precious water from hidden springs, huddled close to a church or protective castle. Thus in the centre of **Robion** on the D2 the remains of an ancient château and a handsome Romanesque church cluster round a turret-shaped

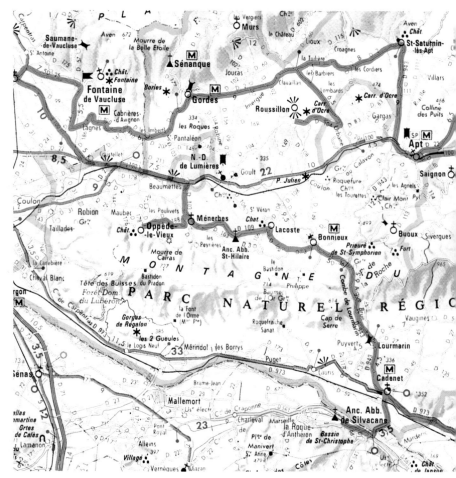

fountain. With the coming of industry many villages were more or less abandoned. Oppède-le-Vieux, reached by the D2, D29 and D176, and ranged at the foot of the impressive ruins of a château and church, is indebted to artists for the restoration of its several 17th- and 18th-century mansions, interspersed with smaller village houses amongst the invading undergrowth clambering up the rocks. In more fertile areas they have planted orchards, but olives and vines always predominate in the traditional agriculture, as at Ménerbes, perched high above neat rows of vine-stocks between a little château and a minor fortress. Continuing along the D109 you pass the abbey of St-Hilaire, then the Château de Lacoste, once owned by the Marquis de Sade, before reaching Bonnieux. Formerly a papal fief, it still has some fine buildings, including the Hôtel de Rouville, now the Town Hall, and some Renaissance works of art in its two churches. To the west, along the D36, then D943, are the Romanesque priory of St-Symphorien, the château at Buoux and a ruined fort.

Heading south again, the D943 crosses the mountains by the Lourmarin pass, reaching Lourmarin village and its Renaissance château which has become the 'Medici villa' of Provence. Next comes Cadenet, with a fine bell tower, a Roman baptismal font, and paintings by the Mignard brothers. Across the Durance the superb Cistercian abbey of Silvacane is worth a detour. At Pertuis on the D973 take a stroll to see the town clock, church of St-Nicolas and in the old quarter the houses of Queen Jeanne III and François I.

The D956 takes you through La Tour-d'Aigues, with its ruins of a Renaissance château, then climbs towards the wooded hills where Grambois has a beautiful church and medieval houses. It runs through Bastide-des-Jourdans, with gates, château, and a pretty chapel and bell tower. Finally you reach Manosque, home of the writer Jean Giono, which has retained a certain charm, with little fountained squares, Renaissance Town Hall and Gassaud mansion, the churches of St-Sauveur and Notre-Dame-de-Romigier, and numerous old houses, doors and gateways. On leaving Manosque, follow the N96 as far as Volx, set on a hilltop crowned with the ruins of a feudal castle, and bear left on the D13. This winds between St-Maime and Dauphin, a medieval village with terraced streets

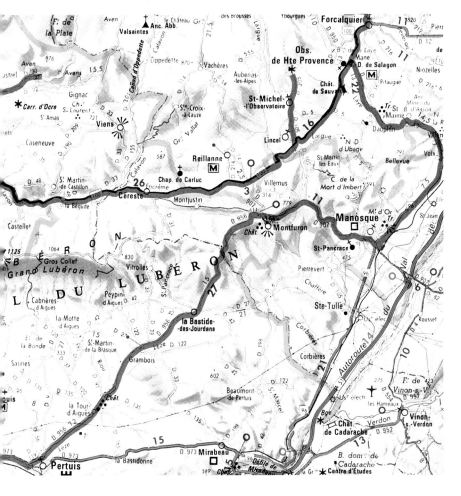

ROUSSILLON, VAUCLUSE

descending the hillside, covered alleyways and ruined ramparts. Next comes **Mane**, built around a medieval fortress, and not far off, one of the loveliest Romanesque churches of Haute-Provence, Notre-Dame-de-Salagon, in the midst of fields.

Here we find ourselves with the Lubéron at our back and facing the distant silhouette of the Montagne de Lure, in the region of **Forcalquier**. The broad levels of plain and plateau rise step by step towards the clear light sky, whilst the first fields of lavender cast their purple shawls across the horizon. The peaceful harmony of the natural scene almost makes one forget the region's glorious past, when Forcalquier was its

ROUSSILLON, VAUCLUSE

capital, as its fine buildings testify: the Convent of the Cordeliers, the church of Notre-Dame-du-Bourget, fine houses and mansions in the rue de Collège, and superb fountain of St-Michel. The N100 takes us down again, making a loop through the pretty village of **St-Michel-d'Observatoire** on the D5, and, if you wish, as far as the Haute-Provence Observatory itself on the D305. Returning on the N100 you skirt the villages of **Reillanne** - with a medieval citadel and 16th-century mansions, **Carluc** - a necropolis and 12th-century priory, and **Céreste** - a medieval village to the north. A few kilometres before Apt, a lane to the left leads to **Saignon**, a picturesque village hemmed in between high cliffs.

Apt is headquarters of the Lubéron Nature Park. The town also boasts the 'Maison du Lubéron' responsible for promoting regional produce and cuisine, together with a museum and exhibition centre. Its architectural jewel is the church of Ste-Anne, regularly embellished and enlarged from the 13th century to the 18th, when the Bishop's Palace was built and the pottery workshops originated. Apt is particularly noted for the marbling effect on its ware. Apt is also famed for its jams, and the D943 to **St-Saturnin-lès-Apt** is lined with cherry orchards. Mainly an agricultural town, St-Saturnin has some fine buildings and the remains of three fortified walls, gates, clock towers and castle ruins. Between Apt and St-Saturnin stretches the so-called 'Colorado' of Provence, where the ochre quarries of Gignac and Rastuel to the east and Gargas and Roussillon to the west, unique in France and mostly abandoned today, offer tourists an almost moon-like landscape of rock and sand in every shade: gold, red, orange, pink and yellow. In the midst of this ochreous landscape **Roussillon**, off the D2 via D227, stands high above cliffs and hills bearing such names as 'Needles of Fairy Glen', 'Cliffs of Blood' and 'Giant's Causeway'. Farther on, by the D102 then D2, is **Gordes**, perched among olive groves and almond trees, with some handsome 16th- and 17th-century houses overlooked by a part-Renaissance château housing the Musée Vasarely. Some 2km north on the D177 is the Cistercian abbey of **Sénanque**, a Romanesque masterpiece. Lanes lead west to the *village noir* or black village, of strange *bories* or field huts built of dry stone. Next comes the village of **Cabrières-d'Avignon** along the D2, then D110, with feudal wall and 16th-century castle. **Fontaine-de-Vaucluse** is well worth a detour by the D100. Here fascinating examples of man's inventiveness combine with the wonders of nature (but avoid the

summer tourist season). After visiting the magnificent Romanesque church of Ste-Marie-St-Véran and the Petrarch Museum, continue along the Sorgue, where the castle ruins cling to its rocky bank. On your way to the 'fountain' you will see, in the middle of the river, the paper-mill belonging to the craft centre of Vallis Clausa. And from the floor of the narrow valley the spring at the source of the river bubbles up, forming a lake and a waterfall. Nine km downstream via the D25 the Sorgue spreads its green watery arms through L'**Isle-sur-la-Sorgue**, encircling the old part of the town. Notice the great mill-wheels in the avenue des 4-Otages, place Emile-Char and the boulevard Victor Hugo. At the centre the hospital and old collegiate church of Notre-Dame-des-Anges have gorgeous interior decoration from the 17th and 18th centuries, when many such private mansions were built. From here the D938 leads back to Cavaillon.

THE MEDITERRANEAN COASTLINE FROM CASSIS TO HYERES

162 km
Map ref
142 E3

A figure-of-eight route with the naval port of Toulon as starting point for both loops. The first part of the tour takes you north-west via the Gorges d'Ollioules and Castellet to the ancient town of Aubagne; then down to the sea at Cassis and back along the coast as far as Sanary. The second loop leads to the marvellous beaches of the Iles d'Hyères, before returning by the Corniche to your starting point. Cassis, La Ciotat and Hyères are the recommended staging posts.

With its arsenal, naval docklands and status as the chief wartime port in France, **Toulon** is in most of its aspects involved with the sea, as shown in the Musée du Vieux Toulon and the Musée Naval. But the heart of the old town, enclosed between the theatre and the Town Hall, offers a timeless picture of the essential fascination of Provence: the bustle of cafés and early morning market, the cool refreshing tingle of the fountains, and, thrown into relief by the crystalline Mediterranean light, the mellow splendour of buildings like the church of St-Louis and the municipal art gallery. This last, incidentally, has an impressive collection of local Provençal paintings, as well as the second largest collection of modern art in France.
Since the 19th century **Ollioules** on the N8 has been involved in the production of flowers, and its Mediterranean flower market, to the south of the town, is the most important in France. Along the rue Pierre-et-Marie-Curie and rue Traversière are passages with medieval porticos. A fortified wall enclosing the ruins of an 11th-century château, and a fortified manor house also lend the place a certain cachet. After passing the Ollioules Gorges, facing you across the Gros Cerveau plateau is the

hilltop village of **Evenos**, on the D462. A little road leads to the hermitage of Vieux Beausset, and the ruins of a fortress and a Romanesque chapel with a statue to the Virgin credited to the Pierre Puget school. **Castellet**, on the D26, overlooks terraced vineyards and olive groves, with narrow covered alleyways leading to the esplanade of the château where the view extends to the Ste-Baume massif. Follow the D2, D1, D3d and the N559 to **Aubagne**, capital of the craft of *santon*-making. Of its ancient ramparts only the Porte Gachiou remains, but along its narrow alleys are the old gates of the 18th-century city. The Tourist Office displays collections of pottery figures, either the Nativity or the 'little world of Marcel Pagnol', a native of Aubagne who used it as the setting for his books.
The old fishing village of **Cassis** on the D1 has a fine 17th-century Town Hall and a medieval castle (private property), while the port and leisure marina are lively with cafés all along the promenade des Lombards. Cassis also has many *calanques*, or creeks, such as those at Port Miou, Port-Pin, En-Vau and l'Oule, where limestone cliffs shelter little sandy or rocky beaches. Previously fringed by aromatic pine forests, the area suffered terribly from fire in 1990 and it will be 30 years before this countryside regains its glory.
The *route des Crêtes*, offering superb views, leads on to **La Ciotat**. Here the old town is centred around the port and the church of Notre-Dame-du-Port, while the rue Abeille and rue des Poilus contain fine 17th- and 18th-century buildings. Beauty spots and bathing places like the creek at Figuerolles, Ile Verte, the Nature Park of Le Mugel and the pebble beach of the Grand

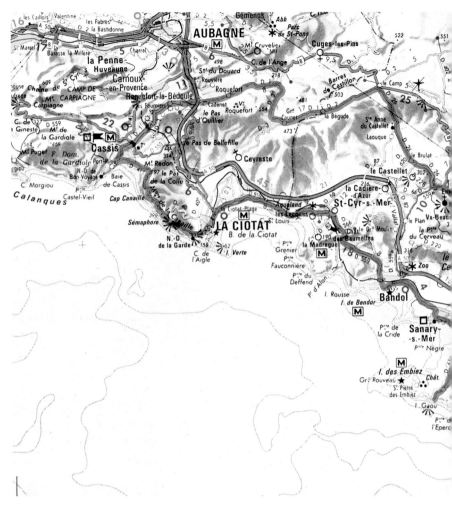

LES CALANQUES

Mugel lie to the west of the bay. Following this bay west to east you reach the seaside resort of Les Lecques and not far away is the archaeological museum of Taurcentum. The D559 continues to **Bandol**, a leisure and walking centre with an old port and marina, the corniche Bonaparte, and the Paul Ricard cultural and sports centre on the isle of Bendor. Beyond the point is **Sanary-sur-Mer**, another charming resort. Small boats link Le Brusc on the D616 with the Ile des Embiez, where the Paul-Ricard Oceanographic Foundation is situated. The D559, leading back to Toulon, passes through **Six-Fours-les-Plages**, with its richly decorated Romanesque collegiate church of St-Pierre-aux-Liens.
From Toulon the Corniche Mourillon, D642 and D559, leads to l'Almanarre, where you follow the old 'Salt Route' to the **Giens** peninsula. Around the hamlet, dominated by the ruins of a château, are the traditional fishing ports of La Madraque and Le Niel. The Tour Fondue is the embarkation port for the island of **Porquerolles**, a natural harbour offering the opportunity of pleasant walks along the coloured cliffs, to the Le Loup gorges, the Le Bregançonnet creek and

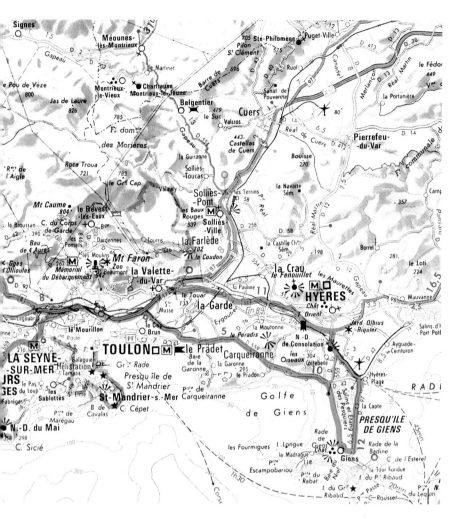

superb beaches (the plages d'Argent,
Blanche, Noire, de la Courtade and
Notre-Dame). Above the Porquerolles
port, the fort of Ste-Agathe houses a
historical and archaeological exhibition of
the Iles d'Hyères.
You reach the Ile de Port-Cros from St-
Pierre-de-la-Mer near Hyères-Plage.
Flora and fauna are protected here by
the Parc National which offers well-
signposted routes on various themes
botanical, marine, flora and fauna, and
includes a visit to the fort.
Returning to St-Pierre-de-la-Mer, follow the
D97 to Hyères, passing the huge tropical
garden of Olbious-Riquier. Hyères marks
the start of the Côte-d'Azur, a great tourist
attraction since 1860 when the revolution in
transport made its gentle winter climate
accessible to a newly rich and cosmopolitan population. Luxury villas appeared along
avenues shaded by palms and oleanders,
like the oriental-style 'Mauresque' and
'Tunisienne' and more recently the avant-
garde 'Villa de Noailles' built around 1924.
Around the place Massillon where the tower
of St-Blaise stands, stretches the old
town, marked out by the gates of its

ILE DE PORT-CROS, VAR

ancient wall: the 13th-century Porte St-
Paul, Porte Barruc and Porte de la
Souquette, 14th-century Porte de la Rade
and Porte Fenouillet. Return to Toulon by
the N98, then the Corniche du Mont
Faron, with stunning views over the sea.

GLIMPSES OF THE ROMAN AND MEDIEVAL PAST

110 km
Map ref
129 D5

A short tour including the important archaeological sites of Orange (the starting point), Carpentras and Vaison-la-Romaine, with medieval and Renaissance villages along the way, some famous 'Côtes-du-Rhône' vineyards, and a detour to Mont Ventoux. Recommended staging posts besides Carpentras and Vaison are Caromb and Malaucène.

Orange with its magnificent Roman amphitheatre and victory arch is one of the most important archaeological sites in Provence. But you will also find a wide range of beautiful buildings which span the centuries. The Cathedral of Notre-Dame-de-Nazareth, built in the 12th century, restored in the 16th and beautified by numerous works of art in the 17th and 18th, is the centre of old Orange, a pleasant place to stroll discovering old houses, picturesque little squares, lovely old

the *Comtat*, with beautiful 15th- and 16th-century fortified gates, 17th- and 18th-century private houses, attractive squares and fountains everywhere. The Ferrande tower with its Notre-Dame door is a most striking building: inside it has superb 18th-century murals depicting the exploits of William of Orange.

To the north-east of Carpentras pretty villages border the D938 as it winds between the vineyards: **Caromb**, 2km off to the right, a walled city whose attractive 14th-century church of Notre-Dame-des-Graces-Saint-Maurice has statues and 15th- and 16th-century paintings; then on to **Le Barroux**, with steep little alleyways running alongside the old houses and dominated by a magnificent 16th-century castle. And finally **Malaucène** where, at the side of its fortified gateway of Soubeyran (one of five still standing), is the 14th-

VINEYARD, VAISON-LA-ROMAINE

gateways and attractive fountains. The municipal museum records the life of the city which has regained its popularity thanks to its celebrated directors of music and theatre.

Reaching **Carpentras**, the old capital of Vénasque, via the D950, you enter by the porte d'Orange gate. In the heart of the town a Roman victory arch with superb carvings of chained prisoners faces the 17th-century Palais de Justice, where many rooms contain fine paintings. On the left is the Gothic cathedral of St-Siffrein, famous for its Flamboyant south door and interior embellished by many works of art. Close by, opposite the Town Hall, stands a magnificent 18th-century synagogue. From the town centre follow the rue des Halles and the rue du Collège to discover the arcades and fine buildings on your way to the museums behind the Palais de Justice.

Pernes-les-Fontaines, due south by the D938, is one of the prettiest little towns in

century church of St-Michel-et-St-Pierrre. Originally built into the surrrounding wall and decorated with machicolation, it now houses a superbly carved 18th-century organ-chest. Follow the old alleyways until you reach the clock tower, then on to the site of the old château from where there are superb views over the mountains. Malaucène is also a good departure point for an optional trip to **Mont Ventoux**: take the D974 and follow it along the ridge to chalet Reynard, then descend through the small hamlets to **Bédoin**. On the other side, to the west, sharp limestone hills, around which are scattered little villages, stretch for 15 km along the border of Montmirail. **Beaumes-de-Venise** on the D90, enclosed by terraced vineyards, is famous for its muscat wines. Beyond the village, on the right, is the Romanesque chapel of Notre-Dame-d'Aubune, and then you follow the 'Wine Route' along the D7 between Vacqueyras and **Gigondas**, where one of

the best Côtes-du-Rhône is produced. The D79 then leads to **Sablet**, once fortified, and the D23 to **Séguret**, a charming village with several very attractive buildings: the Reynier gate, church, belfry and fountain with gargoyles.

Vaison-la-Romaine on the D938 has some important Roman remains in what were the residential quarters of Puymin and La Vilasse, and has preserved two beautiful examples of Romanesque religious architecture: the cathedral of Notre-Dame-de-Nazareth and its cloister, and the chapel of St-Quenin. South of Vaison the 13th- and 14th-century upper city retains its historic layout of cobbled alleyways lined with old houses and dotted with fountains, at the foot of the ruined castle belonging to the Counts of Toulouse.

The D975 carries on down through the vineyards, past **Roaix** and **Rasteau** with its museum of viticulture and then, by way of **Camaret-sur-Aigues**, back to Orange.

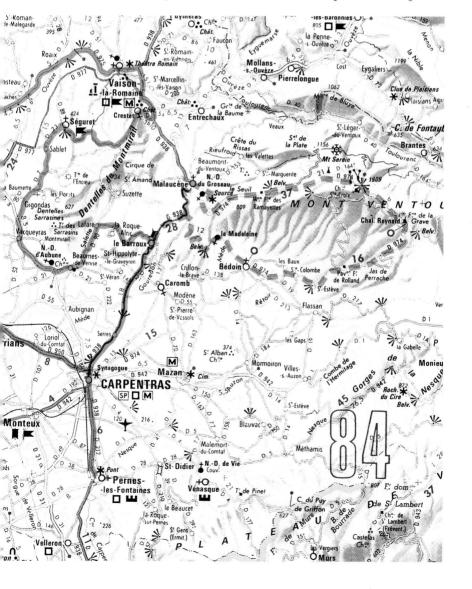

A CIRCULAR TOUR ROUND MARSEILLE

215 km
Map ref
137 D4

From the ancient and typically Provençal town of Aix this tour takes you in a ring through the old and new towns and villages of the Etang de Berre and the Côte Bleue, as well as to Marseille, the second largest city and most ancient port in France. Martigues is recommeded as a staging post if you are not staying in Aix or Marseille itself.

Aix-en-Provence is certainly worth a full day's visit to stroll through its old city which has miraculously preserved many 17th- and 18th-century buildings. Here the atmosphere is one of privilege: a magic little touched by any incursion of busy commercialism. Broad squares, springing fountains and generously-proportioned caryatids, gargoyles and friezes on pale stone façades, or shadowy mouldings on carved doorways to catch the eye. From the busy cafés of the cours Mirabeau (the perfect place for a break), the impressive line of private mansions flank the far side. Look up from the early morning flower

market to the Town Hall bell tower with its statuary and campanile, or turn down from the flamboyant façade of the St-Saveur cathedral to discover the pure, simple beauty of its cloister; or again, at night when the street is deserted savour the fascination of the place d'Albertas.

North-west of Aix the village of Eguilles on the D17 is perched on a plateau at the edge of which stands the charming château of Boyer d'Eguilles. On leaving the village, take the D543 and then D10 to the outskirts of Ventabren, a pretty hilltop village and of Roquepertuse, with its Celto-Ligurian sanctuary.

Reaching the Etang de Berre you follow the bank as far as the Pont Flavien on the right of the road, an arch with foliated scroll pilasters bearing two small carved lions at the top and dating from the 1st century AD. Next you arrive at St-Chamas, an old fishing port with a beautiful Baroque church; then Miramar-le-Vieux, perched on a rocky outcrop around the ruins of a

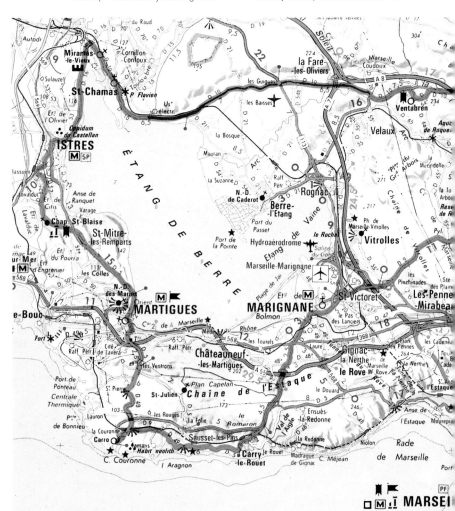

medieval castle. Still skirting the Etang de Berre on the D76, then the Etang de l'Olivier and the Oppidum du Castellan, you enter Istres through the Porte d'Arles, from which streets of winding stairways climb the hill, with glimpses of beautiful 17th- and 18th-century houses, the Grande rues des Fabres, and, flanked by an esplanade, a fortified church. Once through the Porte d'Arles take the allée Jaurès and then place des Carmes to reach the rue du Portail-Neuf and the museum of old Istres. Farther on, along the D52, then D51, on a rise occupied by a Romanesque chapel, lies the important archaeological site of St-Blaise, flanked by a Hellenistic rampart dating from the 3rd century BC. The village of St-Mitre-les-Remparts 3km further on, retains its ramparts, two mills and numerous 17th- and 18th-century houses. The D5 then reaches Martigues which consists of three areas separated by the narrow waterway, the Chenal de Caronte; Ferrières with the Musée Ziem and modern Town Hall on the northern bank, the Ile de Brescon in the

FORT ST JEAN, MARSEILLE

centre and Jonquières with a Baroque church and chapel, and gardens with statues to the south. The island is particularly pleasant with its fine buildings, Baroque church of La Madeleine and its inner channel, known as the 'mirror of birds', where boats throng the quays.
You return to the Mediterranean by the D5, then D49 crossing the chaîne de l'Estaque. From the charming fishing port of Carro follow the *Côte Bleue* by the D49 and D5 - perhaps exploring the pretty beaches at Verdon and le Rouet, and the villages of Sausset-les-Pins and Carry-le-Rouet, once fishing ports now seaside resorts. The D9 leads on to Marignane whose Town Hall is the Château of Marignane with magnificent period decoration. Beyond Vitrolles on the D8 stands the fortified village of Cabriès, then not far from Bouce-Bel-Air on the D60a, the Château d'Albertas, a huge pavilion in a park with statues and ornamental lakes. Here you follow the D8 along the chaîne de l'Etoile as far as Mimet, taking the road on the right which crosses the massif. On the other side, below the mountain, the Musée du Château Gombert houses an exhibition of local art and culture of Marseille, a perfect foretaste to a visit to France's second largest city. Much more lively than its neighbour and rival Aix, Marseille remains relatively unappreciated perhaps on account of its somewhat dubious reputation. It is not easy either to pinpoint its throbbing cosmopolitan identity or discover the treasures hidden in such an enormous place. At the very least, though, you should take the boat trip round the Vieux-Port, and visit the Byzantine-inspired basilica of Notre-Dame-de-la-Gard, from the top of whose rocky pinnacle, 162m high, you get a view of the whole town, the sea and the islands.
Leaving Marseille you reach the village of Allauch, which still boasts four 17th-century mills on the esplanade F. Mistral, one of which houses a collection of old *santons*. Join the D907 and cross the chaîne de l'Etoile at Cadolive, then take the D7 by way of St-Savournin to Mimet. Finally take the D46 through Gréasque to Fuveau, and follow the *route nationale* back to Aix.

A TOUR THROUGH THE VERDON GORGES

156 km
Map ref
138 B2

Starting from Gréoux-les-Bains this circular trip takes you to a series of viewpoints overlooking the spectacular scenery of the winding gorges of the Verdon river, where picturesque villages alternate with impressive strongholds perched high above. Recommended staging posts are Moustiers-Ste-Marie and Castellane.

The little spa town of **Gréoux-les-Bains** is clustered around the foot of a hill topped by a castle said to have belonged to the Knights Templar. Steps lead down through the old quarter and its two ancient gateways (in the rue des Ramparts and rue du Vieil-Horloge), a Romanesque church renovated in Gothic style, and a 17th-century mansion now the Town Hall. This tour follows the D952 all the way to Castellane, travelling along the north bank of the Verdon. Its tributary, the Colostre, cuts across the plateau, lapping at **St-Martin-des-Brômes** and the outskirts of **Allemagne-en-Provence**. In the first of these villages the church has a pyramidal bell tower; the second seems anxious to rival the thick vegetation of the forests, for in the park surrounding the lovely Château de Castellane the local oak mingles with imported exotic species.

Farther on, four Roman columns signal the entrance to the little town of **Riez**, whose industry centres on the traditional crafts of pottery and the manufacture of *santons*, or clay figurines. Its old quarter is pleasantly fringed by a tree-lined walk in gardens that once belonged to the bishop's palace. The Grande Rue boasts beautiful houses constructed in the 16th and 18th centuries. Farther on you come to **Moustiers-Ste-Marie**, famous in the 17th and 18th centuries for its unusual polychrome pottery. Its ceramic museum houses a collection of beautiful pieces and traces the history of the craft which the town has been redeveloping over the past 50 years. You will also notice the very fine 16th-century carved door of the porch to the Notre-Dame-de-Beauvoir chapel. Between Moustiers and Castellane the D952 and the D23 loop gives further views of the gorges from viewpoints at le Galetas, Le Mayreste, le Baou Beni, Gaston Armaret, l'Imbut, le Maugue, Maline l'Estillié, l'Escalès and le Point Sublime.

Above the village of **Castellane** rises a huge rock, 180 metres high, on which the

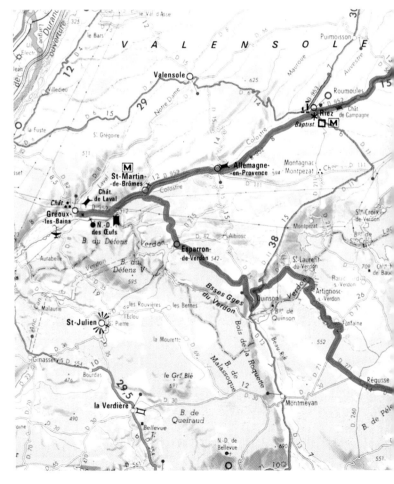

MOUSTIERS FAIENCE

chapel of Notre-Dame-du-Roc perches. Half-way up a pentagonel tower and some ruins mark the site of the old fortifications. Between the Petardiers gate (a passage lined with towers) and the rue du Mitan (a pretty fountain with lions), stands the church of St-Victor, which has a fine 17th-century altar piece and a clock tower surmounted by a bell turret.

South of the Verdon, reached by the D952, D955 and D90, the village of **Trigance**, built like an eagle's nest at the foot of a vast feudal château, presents typical vaulted passages and stairways. Above the roofs appear a tall campanile and the Roman-esque bell-tower with multi-coloured church roof. On the D71, which runs along the 'grand canyon' of the Verdon at the Balcons de la Mescla, you get a series of striking views through the windows of the Fayet tunnel, and, after passing the Corniche Sublime, of the Cirque de Vaumale.

Farther on, the Ste-Croix lake offers a pleasant watersports centre. After the dam, you cross the Verdon and pass through the charming villages of **St-Laurent-du-Verdon**, **Quinson** and **Esparron-de-Verdon** on the way back to Gréoux.

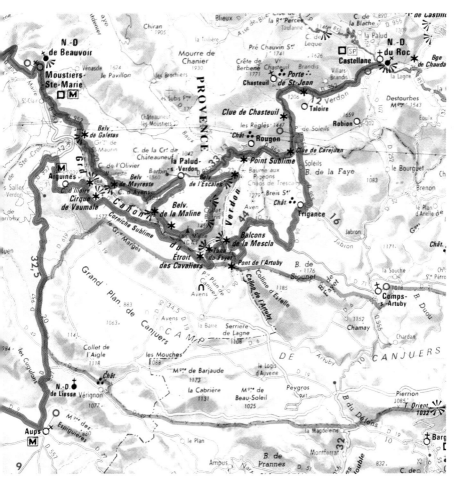

WALKS

This chapter offers a wide and varied selection of itineraries that will help you to get to know Provence and its people by exploring its different regions on foot. The 12 walks range from 4km to 25km in length, most of them being circular tours, with one or two divided into shorter sections which can be combined or taken separately as you please. A few include sections that coincide with waymarked Grande Randonnée (GR) footpaths; some follow motorable tracks for all or part of their distance.

Between them the walks cover many different types of scenery, from the flat marshlands and wide horizons of the Camargue and the rocky inlets and sheltered beaches of the Mediterranean seacoast, by way of medieval hilltop villages perched high above vineyards and olive groves and the fascinating relics of the Roman occupation of Gaul, to the spectacular gorges of the Verdon and the landscapes beloved of artists like Van Gogh and Cézannne. And finally there are windswept mountain crests, like Mont Ventoux, the Grand Montmirail and the Alpine foothills, in some of which there may be an opportunity for rock climbing along the way, for those ready to diverge from the suggested route a little.

The introduction to each walk gives a brief summary of the route, the sort of terrain and countryside, the altitude range and the chief places or features of interest to be visited, as well as the degree of difficulty to be encountered. It also shows how the starting point can be reached by car from one or other of the towns on the appropriate itinerary in the Motoring Tours chapter, where you can branch off for one of the shorter walks, or spend the night before or after the longer ones.

All the maps in this section are 1:25,000 unless otherwise indicated. In order to pinpoint the start of each walk, a map reference has been provided relating to the regional atlas at the back of the book.

LIMESTONE CLIFFS IN THE DENTELLES DE MONTMIRAIL

10 km
Map ref
130 C1

Popular with rock climbers on account of their limestone cliffs, the Dentelles de Montmirail are also a delight for ramblers. This circular itinerary takes in the Dentelles Sarrasines and the Grand Montmirail, before leading back down to your starting point. While in this region famed for its vineyards, be sure to try the fortified aperitif

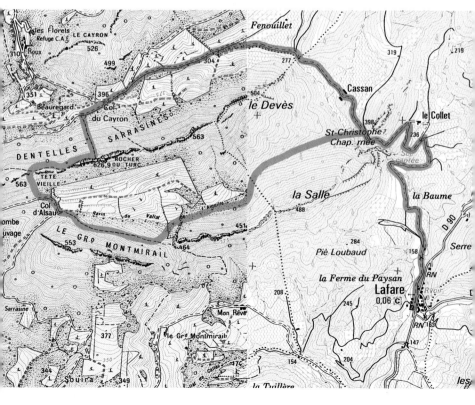

DENTELLES DE MONTMIRAIL

of Rasteau, and the table wines from Gigondas and the Côtes de Ventoux.

This is a walk of moderate difficulty, with an altitude range of 350m, and a few more demanding sections. Access is from Vaison-la-Romaine south-east via the D938. Just before Malaucène take the D90 to the right as far as Lafare, passing below the cirque de St-Amand. On entering Lafare turn right towards Gigondas, to the starting point, the Chapelle-St-Christophe. (The Col de Cayron is accessible by car, but the Chapelle-St-Christophe is preferable as you can park close by.)

From the St-Christophe chapel continue along the road to the Col du Cayron passing close by the Cassan farm. Do not take the paths on your right at the col, but continue for 200m, then take a path leading uphill to the left, which brings you to the Rocher du Turc (627m). Turn right at this point, passing Tête Vieille, and where the path drops away towards Gigondas, cross over the ridge and go down to the Col d'Alsau road. Follow the road as far as the col. Take the path crossing the north flank of the Grand Montmirail, waymarked in yellow. As you approach the rocks of the Lame du Clapis, take the path which drops steeply down to your left into the Vallat de l'Aiguille ravine, still following the yellow waymarks. This path brings you back to your starting point at the Chapelle-St-Christophe.

THE ETANG DE GALABERT IN THE CAMARGUE

25 km
Map ref
135 C4

The Camargue, renowned for its heat, horses, bulls and salt marshes is not a place to be visited during the hottest hours of the day; early morning is preferable for walking. This ramble follows dykes bordering the lakes on the fringes of the national botanical and zoological reserve in the Parc Régional de Camargue.

All at sea level and consisting entirely of tracks accessible to motor vehicles, the route is easy to follow. The starting point is reached from Arles via the N570 towards Les Stes-Maries-de-la-Mer. After Les Passerons take D346 south-eastward along the right bank of the Grand Rhône towards Les Salins-de-Giraud, through Le Sambuc and Péaudure to Le Petit Peloux. Then branch right on to D36c, and at the first junction after St-Bertrand turn left and park 2km farther on, at the side of the Pèbre road, on the approach to the pumping station bridge.

Cross the bridge at the Etang de Galabert pumping station and take the first right.

GARDIAN IN THE CAMARGUE

HORSES IN THE CAMARGUE

Follow this road west for 2km until you come to a place where several ways meet. Take the right-hand track, going first north (the digue d'Amphise), then west. Four km farther on you come to the Pont de la Comtesse. Do not cross the bridge, but take the road due south. Ignore two tracks on your left, but take the third, which leads towards the Beauduc pumping station. Farther on, the track narrows. At the next junction, turn left and, after 1km left again onto a path which takes you back across the étang de Galabert parallel to your outward journey. You will eventually rejoin the route you took earlier, which will bring you back to your starting point.

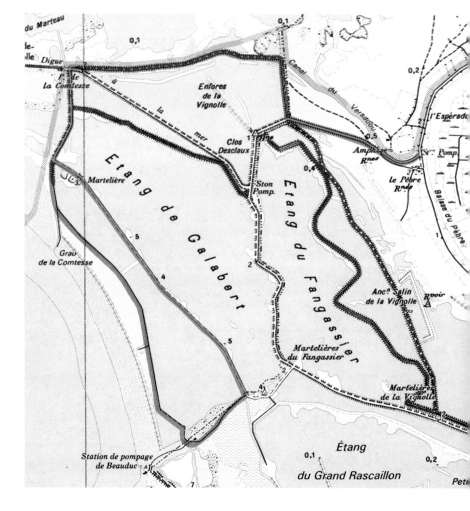

THE CANYON OF THE RIVER VERDON

12 km
Map ref
139 A5

The cliffs of the Gorges du Verdon are a magnet to rock climbers from all over the world, offering many possible climbs. This walk follows the canyon of the Verdon by a path between the river and the cliffs. The itinerary is not circular, so if you have no one to collect you by car you will have to hitch-hike back. If possible, take a torch with you for negotiating the two tunnels along the way, to help you avoid stepping in the puddles. The tunnels also tend to be rather cold.

With an altitude range of about 400m this longish walk between river and cliff involves two tunnels, and a metal ladder which may be a problem for walkers prone to vertigo. Access to the start is from La Palud-sur-Verdon via the D952, following the signs to Castellane. At the junction with the D23 keep left on the D952, and after a few kilometres turn right uphill on the D234, following the Point Sublime signs to the car park at the end of the road.

Access to the end of the walk - if you have someone to collect or you do not want to go all the way back to the start - is also from La Palud-sur-Verdon, where the D23 out of the village runs via the Imbut cliffs to the

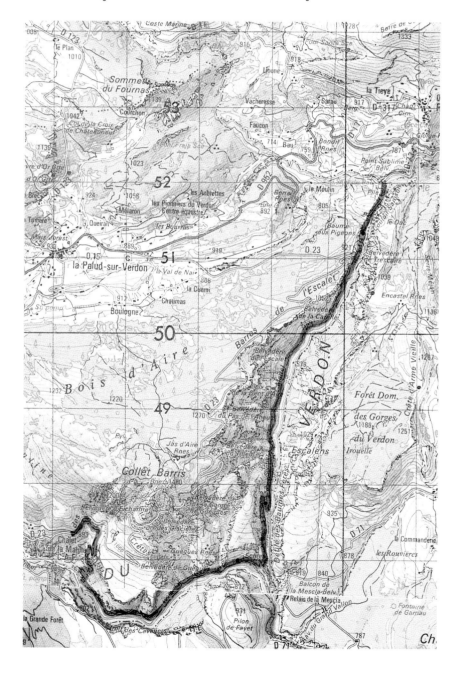

VERDON CANYON

finishing point of the walk at the Chalet-de-la-Maline.

From the car park below the Point Sublime viewpoint, climb down the steps and follow the path along the river. You will encounter two cliff tunnels along the way. The path, which forms part of the Grande Randonnée (GR5) route, continues via ladders to below the Chalet-de-la-Maline. The path then ascends in hairpins. Do not follow the path back down and across the river, but climb right up to the Chalet-de-la-Maline, finishing point of the walk.

THE SUMMIT OF MOURRE NEGRE IN THE GRAND LUBERON

8km
Map ref
137 A4

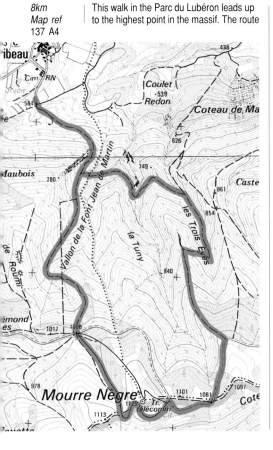

This walk in the Parc du Lubéron leads up to the highest point in the massif. The route describes a large loop, mainly on north-facing slopes - pleasantly cool on hot summer mornings. Needless to say the scents, wildlife and flora of Provence will be among the great pleasures of this walk. With an altitude range of about 650m, from 594m at the starting point of Auribeau to 1,125m at the summit, this tour is definitely one for strong walkers. Access is from Apt via the N100 eastward, turning right on the D48 just before La Bégude and winding in a mainly south-westerly direction through Castellet to Auribeau. At the centre of the village turn left. The walk starts at the end of this road.

Take the path which is a continuation of the road, ignoring paths to the right and left. You will find yourself walking south-eastward, into the valley of la Font-Jean-de-Martin. Climb the valley until you come to a track. Follow it to the left then, a few metres farther on, take a pathway on your right leading to the summit of **Mourre Nègre**. From the summit, follow the path along the ridge line to the east. This brings you back to the track, which continues in an easterly direction. The track eventually leaves the ridge and reaches a point overlooking the combe des Trois Eves. Here, leave the track at a bend and take a pathway leading down to the left. After two hairpins and a straight section (spot height 750m), take the path on your left, which will bring you back to the Font-Jean-de-Martin valley path. From this point, you can retrace your steps to your car.

THE PIC DES MOUCHES AND MONT-STE-VICTOIRE

9 km
Map ref
137 D5

Although the vegetation covering the Montagne-Ste-Victoire was recently devastated by fire, the area is still one of great interest for walkers and rock climbers. The mountain is also, of course, associated with the artist Cézanne (1839-1906), a native of Aix-en-Provence, who painted it from every angle and at every season. Along your path you will find the herbs typical of Provence; try some as seasoning with your meals.

With an altitude range of some 650m between 376m at the starting point and 1,011m at the summit, this is a fairly demanding route, and may be slippery in bad weather. Access is east from Aix-en-Provence and north from Trets to Puyloubier at the foot of the eastern slope of the Montagne-Ste-Victoire which you can enter from the south by the D12.

Start either from the village square or from the upper car park, which is on the left of the street running steeply up from the fountain at the end of the road.

From the car park in the upper village at Puyloubier, join the street running uphill and follow it until you pick up the red and white waymarks of the GR9, which leads all the way to the summit of the Pic des Mouches. Head towards the reservoir and get up onto the ridge. The path is indistinct in places. The red earth can turn to mud and become very slippery in rainy weather. Passing the Oratoire de Malvert, the path follows the ridge up to the Pic des Mouches, highest point of the mountain. From here, you look down on St-Ser, with a magnificent view of the Montagne-de-la-Ste-Baume. The descent is along the same route. If you wish to extend your walk by 2 or 3 hours, you can continue along the ridge past the Pic des Mouches as far as the Croix de Provence. You could then walk right through the Montagne-de-la-Ste-Victoire by way of the fantastic Garagaï cavern.

THE STE-VICTOIRE MOUNTAIN

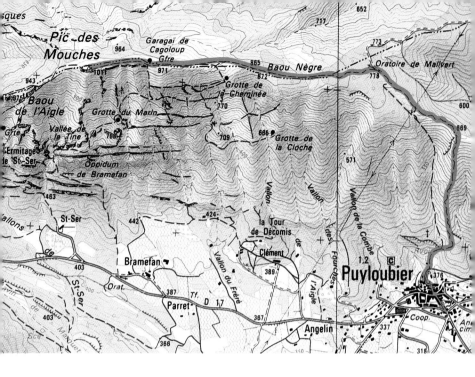

ALONG THE CRESTS OF MONT VENTOUX

14 km
Map ref
130 D3

From the 1,910m vantage point of Mont Ventoux, which gets its name from the winds constantly buffeting its summit, there is a panoramic view over the whole of Provence, as far as the Alps. If you choose a clear day, the eternal snows of the Alpine peaks can be seen standing out sharply against the horizon. Whereas the summer heat makes many walks in the lowland unbearable, up here you will always find cooler temperatures. In winter, when the northern slope is covered in snow, you may still be able to walk on the southern slope - but make sure you wear something windproof.

A fairly high-level route with an altitude range of about 500m between Le Chalet-Reynard at 1,417m and the 1,910m Mont Ventoux summit. Access to the starting point, the car park at Le Chalet-Reynard, near the ski lift, is possible from the summit itself via the D974 on the north slope of the mountain. But arriving from the south, also via the D974, from just north of Carpentras, gives you the bonus of discovering the summit on foot.

From the car park near the ski lift, set off towards **Mont Ventoux** by the road. Three hundred metres after the road junction, branch off onto a path running uphill on the right, which leads to the Tête de la Grave (1,645m). You can take the path parallel with the ridge or, if you are more energetic, follow the ridge line itself to arrive at the Col des Tempêtes. From here, the summit of Mont Ventoux is just a short walk away. The return journey is by a different route, through the splendid pine forest on the southern slope of the mountain. From the summit, take the road downhill to the south side until you come to the first hairpin. On the outside of the bend is a narrow path. This joins a more frequented footpath

leading through the forest and scree to a road below at a place called 'Le Bâtiment'. Turn left onto this road and so back to the starting point of the walk.

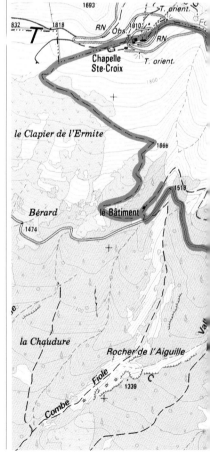

MONT VENTOUX, SUMMIT

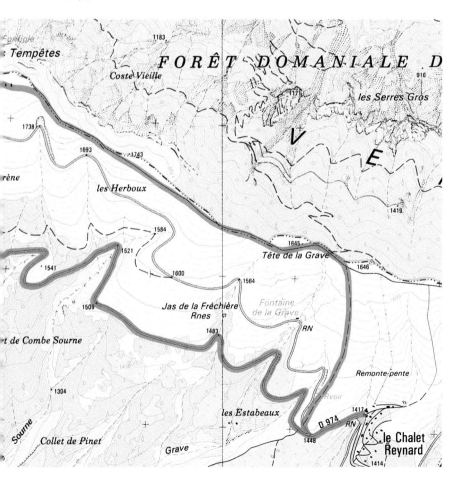

BELOW THE MONTDENIER PEAKS IN THE VERDON AREA

13km
Map ref
139 A5

Though the altitude range is roughly 300m, this itinerary is within the capabilities of anyone able to walk for two and a half hours. If you are tired or your time is limited, you can turn back at any point along the route, having enjoyed an agreeable ramble. Access is from the Lac de Ste-Croix by the winding D952 to La Palud-sur-Verdon, where you branch left on the D123 towards the Col de la Croix-de-Châteauneuf. Cross over the col and continue until the road forks. Branch right and park several hundred metres farther on, where the road becomes a stony track. Continue along the road as fas as the ancient village of Châteauneuf-les-

Moustiers, now in ruins. After the cemetery and the abandoned buildings, continue to follow the road which soon becomes a track, passing below the Rochers de Notre-Dame. Among the rocks near the path you will spot a cave surrounded by low stone walls. You eventually arrive at the Saint Peire bridge, then les Brochiers. At this point, take a path on the right which brings you back to the road near the ruins of les Bondils. This is the farthest point of the walk, with a good view back over the way you have come. For the return, you can simply retrace your steps, or walk back along the road if a car is available to pick you up at les Brochiers.

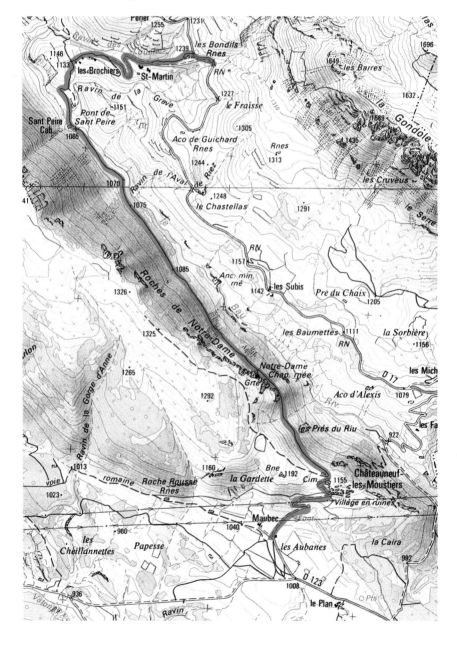

IN THE ALPES-DE-HAUTE-PROVENCE

11 km
Map ref
131 F6

This walk in the Alpes-de-Haute-Provence is sure to whet your appetite for this unspoilt corner of Provence. The biggest village you will encounter, apart from Saumane, is La Tour des Girons, now deserted. While in the region, do not miss

the opportunity to visit the lovely little village of Simiane-la-Rotonde.

The starting point of this tour with an altitude range of 250m, running through unspoilt mountain country, is Saumane, south-west of Sisteron. Access is via the

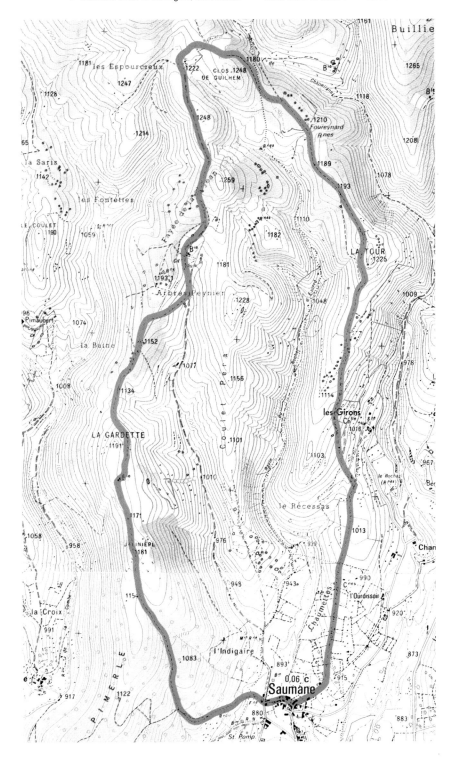

D950 from Forcalquier, heading towards Ongles, and then the D12, following the signposts to Lardiers and then Saumane, where you can leave your car in the village centre.

Take the path which leaves **Saumane** westwards and ascends to the summit of La Gardette. From the top, take the path downhill on the other side, remaining on the ridge of the mountain. Farther on, the path climbs then drops again to join a wide track. Follow this track up through the Fayée-de-la-St-Jean forest, then traverse the mountain to the 1,222m spot height. The route is circular, first following the track, then crossing a clearing and entering the woods again. The path then leads to La Tour des Girons, not climbing right up to the summit but skirting it to the west. Farther on the pathway widens and you leave it on a hairpin bend, where there is a short cut. After climbing gently, the path brings you back down to Saumane by the chemin du Récessas.

CLIFFS, CREEKS AND COVES BY THE SEA

4km
Map ref
141 D4

The little bay of Callelongue cuts into the Montagne de Marseilleveyre, on the headland to the extreme south-west of Marseille. This walk takes in the white limestone cliffs of Les Goudes and its surrounding area, a favourite haunt of rock climbers. Watch out for rock falls caused by their activities on the cliff face. Also, the pass known as the Pas de la Demi-Lune-des-Goudes is exposed and windy. Ranging from sea level at the start to 200m at the Pas de la Demi-Lune, this walk can be tricky on the cliff sections. Access is from Marseille by the coast road south via La Madrague and Les Goudes to the *calanque* of Callelongue.

From the car park at **Callelongue**, take the road into the village. The road continues as a wide dirt track on your left, which will soon bring you to a pathway leading upwards on the right. Take this path, making for the rocky *cirque* which forms the north-west face of the Rocher des Goudes. You will see the wide cleft of the Demi-Lune pass above you. Climb the path on the left-hand side of the cleft, then cross back to the right, taking care with your footing. From here there is a magnificent view of the rocky inlets below. As you follow the base of the cliffs on your left you will also notice that this section is completely sheltered from the Mistral - assuming the Mistral is blowing. When you have taken in the view, turn back through the cleft and take the pathway on your right, hugging the cliffs of the Roc-St-Michel. The caves of St-Michel-d'Eau-Douce and l'Ours are nearby. Cross to the other side of the valley as best you can, and follow the Club Alpin Français (CAF) trail, beneath the south face of the Tête du Trou du Chat, which can be tricky. Having traversed the whole mountainside, you will find a pathway on the left which leads back to the starting point.

TO THE SUMMIT OF THE AMARRON

13 km
Map ref
142 B3

The altitude ranges from 300m at Garéoult near the start to 770m at the Amarron summit. Access is from Brignoles south-east by the D554, skirting Garéoult to the north if you want to avoid the village centre. Take a road to the right past the cemetery and over a bridge to the Bellevue housing development, where you should be able to park. If you go into Garéoult itself, it is worth visiting the church of rough-hewn stone in the centre of the village.

From the place you have parked, walk back to the main road from **Garéoult**. Follow it north-westwards as far as a reservoir at the first left-hand bend. Leave the road here by a pathway on your right, waymarked green, leading up into mixed pine and oak woods. Farther on, the path emerges onto the same motor road you were on earlier. Follow it for about two kilometres and, when it ends, take the track on the left leading to the Amarron ridge and up in a westerly direction to the summit. You can come down the same way, or via the Vallon du Cendrier. In the latter case, continue along the ridge line after the summit. Shortly after the point where the path drops down the southern slope, take the path on your left into the valley. Before emerging from the vallon du Cendrier, take a path branching away left (spot height 390m), which leads to La Bastide Chabert. From here, the road brings you back to your starting point.

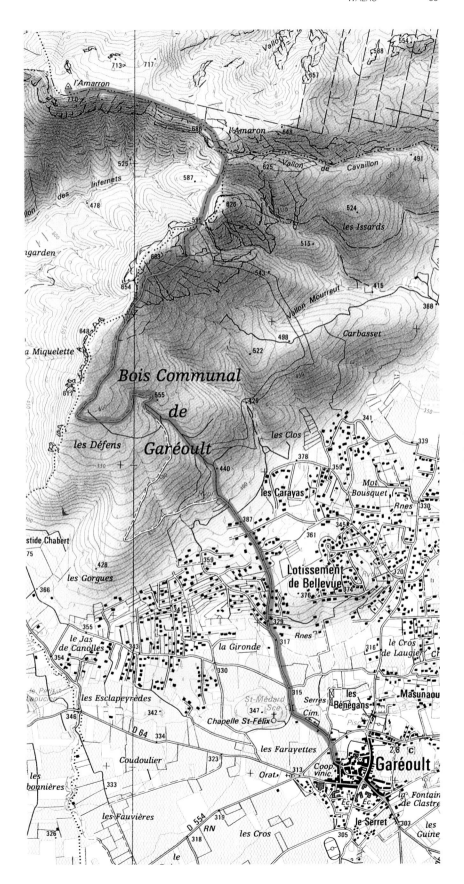

ART AND ARCHAEOLOGY IN THE ALPILLES

6 km
Map ref
135 B5

Many readers will associate St-Rémy-de-Provence with Vincent Van Gogh. So take this opportunity to visit the old town, which has a museum in the Hôtel de Sade, dedicated to the Alpilles, a collection of the archaeological discoveries made at Glanum, and the Van Gogh art centre.
This walk is no higher than 100m, but there are some steep uphill sections and a fixed ladder to negotiate at one difficult point. Access is from Avignon by the N570 then D571 south to the starting point at St-Rémy, where you can park in avenue Pasteur near the Syndicat d'Initiative.
Outside the town there are: two Roman monuments at "Les Antiques" (an arch and a mausoleum), the Roman remains at Glanum, the 12th-century priory where Van Gogh stayed, and the church of St-Paul-de-Mausole. The collegiate church of St-Martin is also worth a visit, for the sake of its interesting organ.
Leave **St-Rémy** southwards by the avenue Van Gogh, the the D5 (GR6) as far as **St-Paul-de-Mausole**. The priory and the remains of **Glanum** are in the immediate vicinity. Continue along the D5 to the first bend, where a path branches off on the right. Take this path uphill, then down again to the Peiroou dam. There is a fixed ladder here to help you over one difficult section. The path follows the bank of the reservoir to the south, bringing you back again to the dam. A path on your left leads to the road, which you follow northwards back to St-Rémy.

THE RUINS AT GLANUM

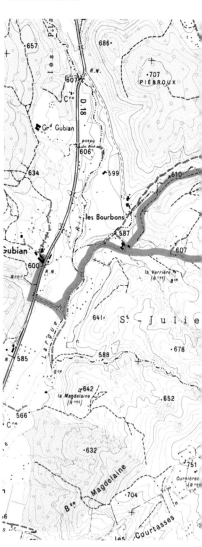

WOODLAND AND WATER NEAR FORCALQUIER

14 km
Map ref
131 E6

A circular walk with virtually no change in altitude. There are a number of possible short cuts along the way, so the itinerary can be varied at will. Mind you do not get lost though. Access is via the D950 west and north from Forcalquier, and then the D13 to the starting point in Limans village. From Limans, take the road north past the cemetery until you come to a junction. Turn left here and continue over the bridge crossing the Praverge ravine and on to Les Bailières. Here you join a wide path leading to Le Pâty (short cut to the return route is possible at this point). Aim for the buildings, then take the path skirting them to the north and go on towards the forest. A small lake is a sign that you are on the right track. North-west of the lake is a pathway which, although it seems to be petering out, takes you through the woodland and eventually to an area of open ground. From here, a wider pathway leads off on the left. Ignoring the first branch to your right, you will come to a parting of the ways (spot height 674m). Take the left-hand fork and after about 1km turn off right. A series of paths brings you to a track which in turn becomes the road to Gubian. Here is an interesting archaeological site and you would do well to find someone who can explain the discoveries made there. The return route runs south of the way you took on the way out. From Gubian, first retrace your steps along the road. After the bridge, turn left. At the first junction, branch left, cross the bridge and follow the path until you come to some buildings. Take the path to the right of them, and continue until the path ends near a pond. You will pick up another path on the left. Follow this until you come to a major meeting of the ways. Here you take a more modest path. The pathway widens and a little farther on joins a road. Paths running parallel to this road lead back to Limans, where you could spend the rest of the day exploring.

GAZETTEER

Set between mountains and sea, Provence is part of the larger region known as Provence-Alpes-Côte-d'Azur. For the purposes of this guide, the area encompassed includes the *départements* of Bouches-du-Rhône, Vaucluse, part of Alpes-de-Haute-Provence, the Var and the Gard - an area which roughly corresponds to the historical notion of Provence.

The A-Z gazetteer section which follows features a selection of the region's top locations; from rural villages of great charm to the great urban centres of interest for their shops, markets and many cultural activities. Each entry contains details on who to contact for sports and other pursuits. Selected hotels, restaurants and camp sites are included, and a host of facts of historical, architectural and general interest to complete your appreciation of this great holiday region.

In fact, all your questions are answered on what to do, what to see and where to go.

LEFT SHEEP ON THE MONT VENTOUX **ABOVE** FEAST OF ST-ELOI

74   *PROVENCE*

AIGUES-MORTES
Map ref 134 D1
Pop 5,000
Nîmes 40 km
Marseille 138 km
Toulon 205 km
Paris 782 km
🛈 place St-Louis
☎ 66.53.73.00

Aigues-Mortes's early prosperity was based on its ancient trades of wine and salt production and its name derives from the Latin *aquae mortuae* meaning dead waters. Today the lively town thrives on tourism. Summer visitors come to explore its unchanged narrow streets and the impressive surrounding walls, as well as to watch the twice-weekly displays of bullfighting or to ride the little Camargue horses. Built by King Louis IX (St-Louis) in the 13th century as a port, the town's importance soon declined; the sailing channels quickly silted up and the sea is now 8 km away. But the fortified walls appear today across the flat coastal plain, very much as they did to the Crusaders departing for the Holy Land.

Hotels
Hôtellerie des Remparts ***
6 place Anatole-France
☎ *66.53.82.77*
(and restaurant)
St-Louis ***
10 rue Amiral-Courbet
☎ *66.53.72.68*
(and restaurant)
Croisades **
2 rue du Port
☎ *66.53.67.85*

Camping
La Petite Camargue
☎ *66.53.84.77*
420 places 27 Apr-21 Sep

Restaurants
La Camargue
19 rue de la République
☎ *66.53.86.88*
La Goulue
2 ter rue Denfert-Rochereau
☎ *66.53.69.45*
Isle de Stel
Canal d'Aigues-Mortes
(facing Tour de Constance)
☎ *66.53.63.75*
(floating restaurant)

AIGUES-MORTES

Modern travellers explore the ramparts and the Constance Tower, with their magnificent views from the Camargue to the Cévennes, take boat trips on the Rhône to Sète canal linked with the Canal du Midi, or use the town as a base for visiting the Camargue.
Leisure
Boat Hire   Houseboats are available for hire at the port base from Locoboat Plaisance ☎ *66.53.94.50*
Boat Trips   Several operators offer canal cruises. Further information from the Tourist Office.
Fishing   Night fishing trips along the canals with Pescalune ☎ *66.53.79.47*
Golf   18-hole public course at Golf de la Grande Motte, 34280 La Grande Motte ; 18-hole private course at Golf Club de Campagne, route de St-Gilles, 30000 Nîmes ☎ *66.70.17.37*
Riding   Mas du Daladel ☎ *66.53.63.65*
Tradition   Reconstruction of St-Louis's departure for the Crusades on the Feast of St-Louis, second half of Aug.
Wine   Visit the cellars at Domaine de Jarras-Listel ☎ *66.53.63.65*

AIX-EN-PROVENCE

Map ref 137 D4
Pop 125,000
Marseille 28 km
Toulon 94 km
Nîmes 109 km
Paris 793 km
🛈 2 place Général-de-Gaulle
☎ 42.26.02.93

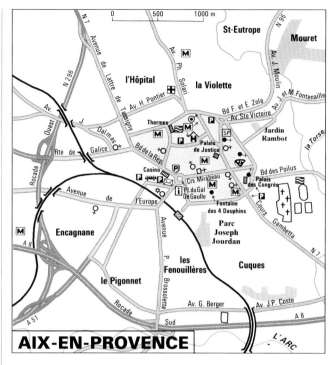

AIX-EN-PROVENCE

Although an important Roman city on the Via Aurelia, Aix later suffered from the constant passage of invaders - Visigoths, Lombards and Saracens - and has no Roman remains. The Middle Ages brought turbulent days of plague, the Hundred Years War and quarrels over succession; peace under Aix's own king, le Roi René, marked the town's golden age of the 15th century. Louis XIV visited Aix and encouraged extravagence and display, visible in the elegant houses built of golden stone with wrought-iron balconies, such as those along the magnificent Cours Mirabeau and other streets. The broad Cours, named after a famous local nobleman-turned-revolutionary, is lined with four rows of plane trees and

Hotels

Le Mas d'Entremont ****
montée d'Avignon, RN7
☎ *42.23.45.32*
(and restaurant)
Pullman le Pigonnet ****
5 avenue du Pigonnet
☎ *42.59.02.90*
(and restaurant)
Hôtel des Augustins ***
3 rue de la Masse
☎ *42.27.28.59*
Caravelle ***
29/31 boulevard du Roi René
☎ *42.21.53.05*
Le Domaine de Tournon ***
Les Pinchinats
☎ *42.21.22.05*
(and restaurant)
Le Manoir ***
8 rue d'Entrecasteaux
☎ *42.26.27.20*
Grand Hôtel Nègre Coste ***
33 cours Mirabeau
☎ *42.27.74.22*
Novotel Beaumanoir ***
Résidence Beaumanoir
avenue des Infirmeries
☎ *42.27.47.50*
(and restaurant)
Mercure Paul-Cézanne ***
40 avenue Victor Hugo
☎ *42.26.34.73*

Camping

Arc-en-Ciel ****
Pont des 3 Sautets
☎ *42.26.14.28*
65 places Apr-Oct

FOUNTAIN, AIX-EN-PROVENCE

punctuated with fountains; one side is devoted to business and banking while the other has the bustle of cafés, brasseries and student life. As usual in Mediterranean cities, much business and social life goes on out of doors until late into the evening, while everywhere the heat of the summer is tempered by deep shade and the fountains' running water. There are more than forty fountains in a wide range of styles: debonair lions, dolphins, eagles, obelisks or Roman pillars with Corinthian capitals. Some are still fed by spring water, such as the warm water flowing out of the Moussue fountain in the cours Mirabeau and the Pascal fountain in cours Sextius where water gushes out from a thermal spring.

This is an unforgettable town with a genuine Provençal atmosphere and in high summer, when the arts festival is staged here, one that is thoroughly cosmopolitan. Aix's modern fame rests on its university and skills in technology and electronics as much as its beauty and its festivals. Among the many churches and impressive public buildings is the cathedral, an amalgam of styles from 5th to the 7th centuries, and the Museum of the Le Vieux-Aix in one of the finest 17th-century private houses, showing relics and discoveries from all periods of the city's past. The Granet Museum houses both classical and contemporary art.

The most famous artist in Aix's history is undoubtedly Paul Cézanne, who was born here and spent all his working life studying and painting Provence. In particular, the bold white peak of the nearby Mont Ste-Victoire appears in many of his paintings, and his studio, open to the public, remains as he left it. Cézanne's mountain has a further notable artistic connection; at its foot is the beautifully situated château of **Vauvenargues**, where Picasso lived.

Leisure

Art Musée Granet houses a notable art collection; the Pavillon Cézanne contains memorabilia of the artist; the Fondation Vasarely, avenue Marcel Pagnol, displays pictures and other works of this modern artist ☎ *42.20.01.09*

Casino place Jeanne d'Arc ☎ *42.26.30.33*

Golf Long and flat 18-hole private course at Golf d'Aix-Marseille, Domaine de Riquetti, 13290 Les Milles ☎ *42.24.20.41; new 18-hole private course at Golf de Fuveau, Château l'Arc, Rousset sur l'Arc, 13710 Fuveau* ☎ *42.53.28.38, with the longest green in Europe, frequent bunkers and stretches of water; private 18-hole course around stretches of water at Golf de Cabriès, 13480 Cabriès.*

Spa Rheumatism/bone joint damage (under renovation) ☎ *42.26.01.18*

Tradition Music and drama festivals throughout the year; international music festival, Jul.

Walking From Le Tholonet follow the Route Paul-Cézanne.

THE VASARELY FOUNDATION, AIX-EN-PROVENCE

Chantecler ****
Val St-André
☎ *42.26.12.98*
240 places open all year
Le Félibrige ***
quartier Beaufort
chemin des Fusains
Puyricard
☎ *42.92.12.11*
100 places Apr-Sep

Youth Hostel
3 avenue Victor Hugo
☎ *42.20.15.99*

Restaurants
Les Semailles
15 rue Bruyès
☎ *42.38.24.64*
Clos de la Violette
10 avenue Violette
☎ *42.23.30.71*
Vendôme
2 bis avenue Napoléon Bonaparte
☎ *42.26.01.00*
Le dernier Bistrot
19 rue des Epinaux
☎ *42.21.13.02*

ARLES
Map ref 135 C4
Pop 51,000
Nîmes 28 km
Marseille 87 km
Toulon 154 km
Paris 755 km
🛈 35 place de la
République
☎ 90.96.29.35

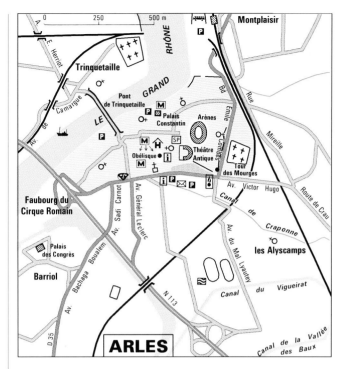

Some of the most outstanding Roman remains in Europe can be explored in the heart of this delightful old town, a place which has inspired creative artists of all kinds. Van Gogh associations abound, for it was here that the artist lived for the last two years of his life, inspired by the buildings and strong light of Provence. For many the name of Arles is linked with Bizet's music for *L'Arlésienne*, his dramatic setting of Daudet's tale of love and tragedy.

Arles was an important Roman town and provincial centre and has retained its magnificent Roman arena - three square towers survive of the later medieval fortifications; the great amphitheatre, restored, is much in use; the Roman baths, *les thermes* and the Alyscamps, a large cemetery of very early Christian origin. The old town is a maze of narrow streets, many lined with elegant Renaissance houses, winding round fine buildings such as the Romanesque church and cloisters of St-Trophime, the 17th-century town hall facing a fountain in the dignified place de la République, the Museon Arlaten created by Frédéric Mistral to illustrate all aspects of Arles life and the Réattu Museum with its collection of works by Picasso, presented by the artist himself.

The Musée Lapidaire Païen, in the former church of Ste-Anne, has Gallo-Roman antiquities, balanced in the Musée Lapidaire Chrétien, in the former Jesuit chapel, by a particularly impressive collection of stonework, tombs from early graveyards evocatively illustrating the skill of 4th-century stonemasons in Arles. To return to the present time and everyday

Hotels
Jules César ****
boulevard des Lices
☎ *90.93.43.20*
(and restaurant)
D'Arlatan ***
26 rue Sauvage
☎ *90.93.56.66*
Atrium ***
1 rue Emile Fassin
☎ *90.49.92.92*
(and restaurant)
Auberge la Fenière
RN 453, Raphèle-les-Arles
☎ *90.98.47.44*
(and restaurant)
Les Cabanettes ***
RN 572, route des Cabanettes
☎ *66.87.31.53*
(and restaurant)
Du Forum ***
10 place du Forum
☎ *90.93.48.95*
(and restaurant)
Mas de la Chapelle ***
petite route de Tarascon
☎ *90.93.23.15*
(and restaurant)
Mireille ***
2 place St-Pierre
☎ *90.93.70.74*
(and restaurant)

Camping
Crin Blanc ***
CD 37, Hameau de Saliers
☎ *66.87.48.78*
180 places Mar-Sep

THE ST TROPHIME CLOISTER, ARLES

Les Rosiers **
Port-de-Crau
☎ *90.96.02.12*
150 places Apr-Oct
La Bienheureuse **
Raphèle-les-Arles
☎ *90.98.35.64*
65 places open all year

Youth Hostel
20 avenue Foch
☎ *90.96.18.25*

Restaurants
Vaccarès
9 rue Favorin
☎ *90.49.06.17*
Côté Cour
65 rue A-Pichot
☎ *90.49.77.76*
L'Olivier
1 bis rue Réattu
☎ *90.49.64.88*
Hostellerie des Arènes
62 rue Refuge
☎ *90.96.13.05*

activity, the boulevard des Lices, an attractive street lined with plane trees, is the place to stroll and observe Provençal life. In addition to summer drama and folk festivals staged in the ancient theatre, Spanish bullfights are held in the arena in July and September, and Provençal-style bullfights from Easter onwards.

Arles lies at the mouth of the wild salt marshes of the **Camargue**, a vast nature reserve famous for its white horses and flocks of pink flamingos. Many excursions visit this area, a delight for riders, walkers and painters, although increasingly encroached on by the expanding rice fields and vineyards.

Leisure
Art Musée Lapidaire Païen, church of Ste-Anne; Museon Arlaten, Musée Lapidaire Chrétien, Hôpital de Laval-Castellane; Musée Réattu.

Boat Trips on the Rhône.

Bullfights in the arena, some Sundays, Apr-Oct; petite Corrida 15 Aug, grande Corrida, Easter and early Sept.

Golf 18-hole public course at Golf de Servanes, Domaine de Servanes, 13890 Mouriès ☎ 90.47.59.95; two 9-hole public courses at Golf des Baux de Provence, Domaine de Manville, 13520 Les Baux-de-Provence ☎ 90.54.37.02

Photography International fair, July.

Tradition Rice Fair and Grape Harvest Feria, mid Sept.

AUBAGNE
Map ref 133 C5
Pop 38,500
Marseille 16 km
Toulon 67 km
Nîmes 141 km
Paris 835 km
🛈 esplanade de
Gaulle
☎ 42.03.49.98

Aubagne is perhaps best known as the birthplace of Marcel Pagnol, 1895-1974, who has left a warm, affectionate but realistic portrait of life in rural Provence and Marseille, both as fiction and as memoirs. He wrote many books, plays and films, and his work is constantly revived or the films remade; these include *Jean de Florette*, *Manon des Sources*, *Marius*, *Fanny* and *La Gloire de Mon Père*. The countryside around Aubagne and round the nearby *mas* where he lived for much of his life, can still provide a sound illustration of the challenges of peasant life amid this beautiful scenery. Those who have enjoyed his work may well enjoy visiting the scenes of his childhood, identifiable from his books, in the countryside around Aubagne as well as in Marseille where he lived as an adult. Other well-known local personalities are the *santons*, the little earthenware figures of ancient tradition, delicately moulded and dressed in Provence costume and used to decorate the crib at Christmas. They make very popular souvenirs. Traces of the town's medieval ramparts are still visible, and the Porte Gachiou is the surviving reminder of the old town's seven entrances. Aubagne is the headquarters of the French Foreign Legion, and there is a small museum here of memorabilia and documents.

Leisure
Golf 18-hole private course at the Golf Country Club La Salette, Impasse des Vaudrans, Quartier de la Valentine, 13011 Marseille ☎ *91.27.12.16. See also Aix-en-Provence.*
Tradition Festival du Rire (laughter) in Jul.

Hotels
*Hostellerie de la Source ***
St-Pierre-Les-Aubagne
☎ *42.04.09.92*
(and restaurant)
*Manon des Sources ***
route d'Eoures
☎ *42.03.10.31*
(and restaurant)
*Hôtel Café du Commerce ***
4 cours Maréchal Foch
☎ *42.03.13.66*

Camping
*Claire Fontaine ***
route de la Tulière
☎ *42.03.02.28*
66 places open all year

AVIGNON
Map ref 129 F5
Pop 92,000
Nîmes 42 km
Marseille 94 km
Toulon 158 km
Paris 722 km
🛈 41 cours Jean
Jaurès
☎ 90.82.65.11

Immortalized in nursery rhyme and more familiarly known as the "Pont d'Avignon", the legendary Pont St-Bénézet still attempts to cross the Rhône though only four of the original twenty-two arches remain; the rest were destroyed by acts of wilful vandalism in times past or through the effects of serious flooding. More impressive is the Palais des Papes or Papal Palace, which acted as fortress, residence and centre of Christendom when a succession of popes held court here during the 14th century. This period was one of huge transformation for the small town, Petrarch describing it as being like the "sewers of the earth". But unsavoury though many of its aspects may have been, it was for the papal patronage of the arts that we can now appreciate Avignon, one of the great art cities of France.
The Palace is really two palaces in one; the 'old' one built for Benoît XII (1335-1342), the 'new' one consisting of additions required for the more lavishly inclined Clement VI (1342-1352). There are cloisters, chapels, private apartments and public audience chambers; rooms where kings and princes were entertained, prisoners held, ecclesiastical matters deliberated or meals prepared. It is an

Hotels
*Hôtel d'Europe ****
12 place Crillon
☎ *90.82.66.92*
(and restaurant)
*Hostellerie les Frênes ****
avenue des Vertes-Rives
Montfavet
☎ *90.31.17.93*
(and restaurant)
*Hôtel Bristol Terminus ***
44 cours Jean Jaurès
☎ *90.82.21.21.*
(and restaurant)
*Hôtel Cité des Papes ***
1 rue Jean Vilar
☎ *90.86.22.45*
*Hôtel Mercure Palais des Papes ***
rue Ferruce, quartier de la Balance
☎ *90.85.91.23*
*Hôtel du Midi ***
25 rue de la République
☎ *90.82.15.56*
*Hôtel Novotel Avignon Sud ***
route de Marseille
☎ *90.87.62.36*
(and restaurant)

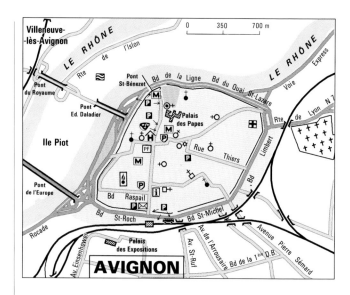

imposing Gothic edifice which, if for no other reason, should be visited for its outstanding 14th-century frescoes.

Not surprisingly, the riches of this ancient ramparted city have led it to become a major commercial and tourist centre; a number of museums and some magnificent secular and religious architecture present a bewildering choice. A small tourist train offers two circuits of interest for the foot-weary.

Leisure
Art Palais des Papes, place du Palais ☎ 90.86.03.32, open daily; Musée de Petit Palais, place du Palais ☎ 90.86.44.58, closed Tues; Musée Calvet closed till 1992 but works transferred to Musée Lapidaire,

Camping
Municipal ****
St-Bénézet
Ile de la Barthelasse
☎ 90.82.63.50
900 places Mar-Oct
Bagetelle ***
Ile de la Barthelasse
☎ 90.86.30.39
360 places open all year.
Les Deux Rhônes **
chemin de Bellegarde
Ile de la Barthelasse
☎ 90.85.49.70
100 places Mar-Dec

Restaurants
Hiély Lucullus
5 rue de la République
☎ 90.86.17.07
Brunel
46 rue Balance
☎ 90.85.24.83
Trois Clefs
26 rue Trois Faucons
☎ 90.86.51.53
St-Didier
41 rue Saraillerie
☎ 90.86.16.50
Le Grangousier
17 rue Galante
☎ 90.82.96.60
Les Grands Bateaux de Provence
allées Oulle
☎ 90.85.62.25
(dine and cruise)

THEATRE, AVIGNON

27 rue de la République ☎ 90.85.75.38,
closed Tues; Musée Louis Vouland, rue
Victor Hugo ☎ 90.86.03.79, closed Sun
and Mon.
Boat Trips Operate from Port de
Plaisance, quai de la Ligne ☎ 90.85.65.54
Cave Exploration Groupe d'Exploration
Souterraine, 9 rue Albert-Camus, 84000
Avignon.
Cycling Cycles can be hired from the
SNCF station.
Golf 18-hole private course, open to the
public, at Golf de Châteaublanc, route de
Châteaublanc, 84310 Morières-les-
Avignon ☎ 90.33.39.08; 18-hole private
course at Golf Grand Avignon, les Chênes
Verts, B.P. 121, 84270 Vedène
☎ 90.31.49.94; 18-hole private course at
the Country Club de Saumane, Domaine
de Goult, 84800 Saumane ☎ 90.20.20.92
Guided Tours Open-sided tourist trains
circuit part of the city and run every half
hour, Easter-Oct.
Riding Pony Club de la Barthelasse,
chemin de Mont-Blanc, La Barthelasse
☎ 90.85.83.48
Tradition Festival d'Avignon (theatre) mid-
Jul to mid-Aug.

BANDOL
Map ref 142 E1
Pop 6,800
Toulon 24 km
Marseille 50 km
Nîmes 162 km
Paris 858 km
🅹 allée Vivien
☎ 94.29.41.35

Bandol's climate, with 320 sunny days
each year, its sandy beaches sheltered by
wooded hillsides, and its wines combine to
make this pretty town a popular resort
throughout the year.
The main promenade is lined with palms
and eucalyptus, the harbour is full of
yachts, and there are good walks in all
directions with fine views. The writer
Katherine Mansfield made Bandol her
home and wrote *Prelude* here. Tourism and
its amenities have added to the town's
prosperity, originally based on its thriving
wine trade, and the two come together on
the Ile de Bendor just offshore. Here Paul
Ricard, the pastis millionaire (pastis being
the famous aniseed-based aperitif), has
created a holiday centre with many
amenities (watersports, diving, walking and
riding), and a museum of wines and spirits.
He is also responsible for the power-boat
complex on the Iles des Embiez.
Sanary, 4 km to the east, is of interest for
its botanic gardens with exotic birds such
as flamingos and storks as well as tropical
plants and fantastic displays of flowering
Mediterranean shrubs.

Leisure
Beach Three sandy beaches with full
watersports facilities.
Casino 24 rue de la République, open all
year ☎ 94.29.45.88
Cycling Cycles can be hired from the
SCNF station.
Museum Musée de la Fondation
Océanographique Ricard, Ile de Bendor.
Zoo Jardin Exotique, situated between
Bandol and Sanary, is particularly
recommended for children.

Hotels
L'Ile Rousse ****
boulevard L. Lumière
☎ *94.29.46.86*
(and restauarant)
Hôtel de la Baie ***
62 rue du Docteur Marçon
☎ *94.29.40.82*
Hôtel Délos Palais ***
Ile de Bendor
☎ *94.32.22.23*
(and restaurant)
Hôtel le Provençal ***
rue des Ecoles
☎ *94.29.52.11*
(and restaurant)
Hôtel la Réserve ***
route de Sanary
☎ *94.29.42.71*
(and restaurant)
Hôtel Ker Mocotte ***
rue Raimu
☎ *94.29.46.53*
(and restaurant)

Camping
Camping du Val d'Aran ***
quartier du Pont d'Aran
☎ *94.29.56.18*
460 places open all year
Vallongue **
route de Marseille
☎ *94.29.49.55*
90 places Apr-Sep

Restaurant
Auberge du Port
9 allée J-Moulin
☎ *94.29.42.63*

THE TROUBADOURS

From the late 11th century until the end of the 12th century the courts of the kings and great nobles of the South of France echoed to the sound of troubadours' poetry and singing. From the Atlantic to the Alps, Provençal was the language of their songs and of those who made them welcome.

The troubadours, of noble or humble birth, composed their works essentially on the theme of courtly love (the *'fin amors'*), an original concept of love based on an idealized image of women. The poet glorified the lady of his choice and analysed his feelings, the torments associated with his love; the virtue of the beautiful loved one aroused joy and inspired the moral perfection of the lover.

This was highly elaborate poetry, both in the richness of its verse and in its devotion to skilful exploration of the human heart. Such refinements contrasted with the other diversion, of a rougher nature, practised by these same troubadours, such as tourna-

A TROUBADOUR PLAYING THE LYRE

ments or hunting. Among the 12th-century troubadours of Provence were Rimbaud de Vaqueiras (protégé of Guillaume IV of Les Baux and subsequently of the Marquis de Montferrat), Rimbaud d'Orange, prince and poet, and Folquet de Marseille, with the most famous generally coming from the south-west. In the 13th century the Albigensian Crusade brought more of them to the courts of Provence, but this very fact also brought about the inevitable decline of the movement.

LES BAUX-DE-PROVENCE

Map ref 135 B5
Pop 400
Arles 19 km
Nîmes 45 km
Marseille 79 km
Toulon 143 km
Paris 754 km
🛈 la Mairie
☎ 90.54.34.39

The history of Les Baux (meaning escarpment in Provençal), perched on its barren rocks, is a strange mixture of elegance, violence and outlaws. The defiant warlords who lived here - who claimed descent from Balthazar, one of the three Wise Men - turned the site's natural defences into a series of fortresses. In the 12th and 13th centuries it was the setting for a "Court of Love", a brilliant society of ladies and their lords and wandering troubadours.

In the 14th century the site fell into the hands of Raymond-Louis de Beaufort, Vicomte de Turenne, who used Les Baux as a base for marauding, looting and taking hostages. Any prisoner unable to raise the ransom demanded was thrown from the castle top to his death at sunset. Cardinal Richelieu put an end to this nest

Hotels
L'Oustau de Baumanière ****
☎ 90.54.33.07
(and restaurant)
La Cobro d'Or ****
vallon de la Fontaine
☎ 90.54.33.21
(and restaurant)
Bautezar ***
Grande rue Frédéric Mistral
☎ 90.54.32.09
(and restaurant)
La Benvengudo ***
vallon de l'Arcoule
☎ 90.54.32.54
(and restaurant)
Mas d'Aigret ***
route Départemental 27a
☎ 90.54.33.54.
(and restaurant)

LES BAUX-DE-PROVENCE

of brigands. The fortifications were dismantled and the village was almost entirely abandoned until the present-day increase in population, largely dependent on tourism. The remains of a few Renaissance houses along the steep and rugged little streets include some very careful restoration. Amongst them are the Hôtel des Porcelets which houses the Museum of Contemporary Art, the Hôtel des Manvilles with a tiny Protestant chapel, and St-Vincent's church high up in the rocks, overlooking an elegant small square. The 13th-century *donjon* provides magnificent views to Arles and the Camargue, even as far as Aigues-Mortes in clear conditions.

In high summer it can be overfull of tourists, but at dusk the dramatic and slightly sinister qualities of this unique place are still apparent.

Leisure
Golf 18-hole public course at Golf de Servanes, Domaine de Servanes, 13890 Mouriès ☎ 90.47.59.95; two 9-hole public courses, Golf des Baux de Provence, Domaine de Manville, 13520 Les Baux-de-Provence ☎ 90.54.37.02

Restaurants
Berengère
rue Trencat
☎ *90.54.35.63*
La Riboto de Tavan
Val d'Enfer
☎ *90.54.34.23*

BOLLENE
Map ref 129 B5
Pop 12,000
Orange 20 km
Nîmes 74 km
Marseille 141 km
Toulon 206 km
Paris 669 km
i place de l'Hôtel de Ville
☎ 90.30.14.43

At the northernmost point of the *département*, contrasts abound here - from the ultra-modern nuclear power station at Tricastin to the troglodyte cave-dwellings at **Barry**. Probably prehistoric in origin, and perfectly placed for avoiding the effects of the Mistral wind while keeping observation across the Rhône valley, they were still in use during the First World War as shelters and hiding places. The area makes a fascinating walk.

Although the old centre is typically Provençal in character, the town extends quite some distance along the banks of the river Lez, with many pleasant open green spaces. There are some surprises too. Recalled in street names, sculpture and a small museum, it was while staying here in 1882 that Louis Pasteur discovered the method of treating the lethal swine fever virus.

It is worth walking to the view point at the top of the town to take in the extensive views of the plains of the Rhône delta, the scrubland of Languedoc to the south and the mountains of the Cévennes away in the distance. The extraordinary site of the nearby fortified village of **Mornas** was militarily important during the 12th century and its spectacular cliffside drop was the scene of some horrible plummeting deaths during the religious wars of the 16th century.

Leisure
Tradition Festival le Papegai, 16th-century costume fair, fourth Sat in June; drama, Jul-Aug; fairs mid Aug, mid Nov.
Walking Local itineraries available from the Tourist Office.
Watersports Sailing, windsurfing and fishing on the 24-ha lake, Trop Long

Hotels
Relais de la Belle Ecluse ***
42 avenue Emile Lachaux
☎ *90.40.09.09*
(and restaurant)
Campanile **
avenue Théodore Aubanel
☎ *90.40.44.44*
(and restaurant)
Le Chêne Vert
quartier St-Pierre
☎ *90.30.53.11*
(and restaurant)

Camping
La Barry ****
quartier St-Barry
☎ *90.30.13.20*
100 places open all year
Municipal du Lez **
quartier des Jardins
☎ *90.30.16.86*
70 places Apr-Sep

Restaurant
Hostellerie du Mas des Grès
route de St-Restitut
☎ *90.30.10.79*

84   PROVENCE

CARPENTRAS
Map ref 130 E1
Pop 25,000
Orange 23 km
Nîmes 68 km
Marseille 102 km
Toulon 166 km
Paris 714 km
🛈 170 allées Jean
Jaurès
☎ 90.63.57.88

The lively energy of Carpentras is seen at
its best on Fridays, when the enormous
general market takes over the town, filling
the narrow lanes within the boulevards that
indicate the line of its medieval town walls.
The surrounding hills provide shelter from
the Mistral, and visitors can appreciate the
sunny Provençal landscape. There are
many beautiful and recently restored old
houses to discover in the town centre.
Much was destroyed, however, between
the time of the Romans and the Avignon
popes (although a triumphal arch remains)
but later prosperity saw a Gothic cathedral
replace the ruined Romanesque church of
St-Siffrein. It incorporates the porch of the
older church, with the curious 'rat ball', a
globe gnawed by rats, of entirely unknown
origin; the church also contains some fine
items in its Treasury.
Other buildings to see include the fine
Renaissance town hall, the synagogue (the
oldest in France), and the magnificent
Hôtel-Dieu. This, still a hospital, was the
creation of an 18th-century bishop,
Malachie d'Inguimbert, who also founded
the Inguimbertine Museum.
At his death he bequeathed his great
library to the town, and visitors to the
Musée Comtadin-Duplessis, housed in the
Italianate Hôtel d'Allemand, can see his
great collection which includes auto-
graphed scores of Bach, Brahms and
Schumann.
The well-irrigated landscape round
Carpentras is cultivated for its fruit, and
charming small towns such as Pernes-les-
Fontaines, with its thirty-three fountains,
and Vénasque are worth seeking out.
Leisure
*Aerial Sports Flying ☎ 90.63.01.41;
gliding ☎ 90.60.08.17
Art Centre Culturel et d'Artisanat d'Art,
rue Cottier ☎ 90.63.46.35
Cycling Cycles for hire from Terzo Sports,*

Hotels
L'Univers ***
place Aristide Briand
☎ 90.63.00.05
(and restaurant)
Safari Hôtel ***
route d'Avignon
☎ 90.63.35.35
(and restaurant)
Le Coq Hardi **
36 place de la Marotte
☎ 90.63.00.35
(and restaurant)
Le Fiacre **
153 rue Vigne
☎ 90.63.03.15

Camping
Municipal de Villemarie **
avenue du Camping
☎ 90.63.09.55
70 places Mar-Nov
Camping du Brégoux
chemin du Vas
Aubignan
☎ 90.62.62.50
175 places Mar-Oct

Restaurants
Saule Pleureur
route d'Avignon
Monteux
☎ 90.62.01.35
La Rapière du Comtat
47 boulevard du Nord
☎ 90.67.20.03
Le Calypso
125 boulevard Alfred-Rogier
☎ 90.60.31.10
Vert Galant
12 rue Clapiès
☎ 90.67.15.50

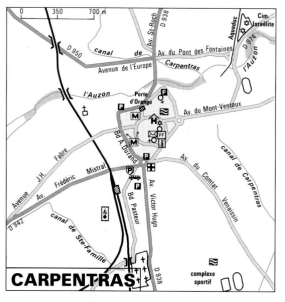

CARPENTRAS

boulevard Gambetta
☎ 90.67.31.56
Golf See Avignon.
Museums *Comtadin Regional Museum
and Musée Lapidaire, archeology,
mineralogy and Musée Sobirats,
decorative arts* ☎ 90.63.04.92
Riding *Trekking Cours du Nord, Camaret*
☎ *90.37.20.26; Ranch de l'Etalon Blanc,
Entraigues* ☎ *90.83.17.68; Manade des
Jonquiers, Mazan* ☎ *90.69.84.76; Centre
Equestre St-Panchan* ☎ *90.60.08.40*
Tradition *Truffle market, Fri mornings in
Jan, Feb, Nov, Dec. Music Festival, mid-Jul
to mid-Aug* ☎ *90.63.16.24; Wine Festival,
end of May.*
Watersports *Also walking and fishing -
for further details enquire at the Tourist
Office.*

TRIUMPHAL ARCH, CARPENTRAS

CASSIS
Map ref 141 D5
Pop 6,500
Marseille 22 km
Toulon 52 km
Nîmes 140 km
Paris 836 km
🄳 place Baragnon
☎ 42.01.71.17

Cassis is a small picturesque fishing port
and village set in a semi-circular bay
against a backdrop of limestone hills and
close to the dazzlingly pretty inlets known
as the **Calanques**. It is, not surprisingly,
extremely popular as a summer resort, and
there is nothing new in this tradition - the
Romans built luxury villas here, and many
of its finest houses date from the 17th
century when citizens of Marseille would
come here to escape the heat of the city in
the summer.
Cassis produces fine red and rosé wines,
and high quality stone from the quarry at
Port Miou nearby. This was the source of
great prosperity when the Suez Canal was
under construction, demanding large
quantities of stone. This fine white stone is
evident all around, for example on the cliffs
of Cap Canaille, the highest in France,
which rise sheer from the sea. The drive
along this cliff-top is steep, dramatic and
unprotected by barriers - not for the faint-
hearted. Down at sea-level, Cassis and the

Hotels
Les Jardins du Campanile ***
*rue Auguste-Favier
route de Marseille*
☎ *42.01.84.85*
(and restaurant)
La Plage Bestouan ***
plage du Bestouan
☎ *42.01.05.70*
(and restaurant)
Hôtel de la Rade ***
1 avenue des Dardanelles
☎ *42.01.02.97*
Les Roches Blanches ***
*route Port Miou
avenue Dardanelles*
☎ *42.01.09.30*
(and restaurant)
Cassital **
place Clémenceau
☎ *42.01.83.44*
Le Golfe **
quai Barthélémy
☎ *42.01.00.21*

CALANQUE, CASSIS

FOREST FIRES

September 1989: the Ste-Victoire forest caught fire and within a few hours the landscapes painted by Cézanne were reduced to ashes.

Tens of thousands of hectares (the average for the last ten years has been 30,000 ha) of Mediterranean woodlands are burnt each year, bringing temporary distress to elected representatives and the general public.

This is not, however, a recent phenomenon. Napoleon I wrote to one of his Préfets:

"I hear that several fires have broken out in the département whose administration I entrusted you. I order you to shoot on the spot the individuals convicted of lighting these fires. Furthermore, if more such fires break out, I shall certainly replace you".

In 1869, Faré, Director General of Water and Woodlands, came to enquire into the serious fires affecting the Maures and Esterel massifs. The Masson encyclopaedia reports that between 1890 and 1900 a considerable number of woodlands caught fire, in particular near Marseille and at Carpiagne, Luminy and Marseilleveyre.

With its dry climate during the long summer months, Provence is more exposed to this risk than other French regions, and the Mistral wind fans the flames through the brushwood from tree to tree. The original cause of a fire may be accidental or criminal - fire raisers, property developers (according to some Parliamentary deputies) but, most often, the carelessness of tourists or local inhabitants.

More or less effective preventive measures remain the best means of dealing with this menace, the surest methods being:

clearance, which may be natural, with the assistance of a herd of goats, or mechanical which may itself occasionally cause an outbreak of fire, as happened at Ste-Victoire;

the creation of trench firebreaks, halting the onward sweep of the flames;

fire-watching, so that outbreaks of fire can be dealt with before they get out of control;

supplies of water points and access roads for fire-fighting vehicles. When fire is discovered, it is the local firemen who are responsible for dealing with it, with the help of their small fleet of "Canadair" water-bombing aircraft which scoop the water out of the sea and drop it on their burning targets.

The ravages of fire are not irreversible, but the Ste-Victoire mountain will need thirty years and ten million francs to restore it to the state which Cézanne knew.

Calanques have attractive beaches and rocks suitable for bathing. This is a beautiful but very vulnerable stretch of coastline, with evidence of the destruction wrought by recent fires sadly visible. Great vigilance is essential for its future protection.

Leisure

Boat Trips By mini-subs to the Calanques
☎ *91.06.99.35*
Casino avenue Lerich ☎ *42.01.78.32, open all year.*
Golf 18-hole public course at Golf Country Club at the Club de la Salette, Impasse des Vaudrans, la Valentine, 13011 Marseille ☎ *91.27.12.16*
Tradition Water festival, 29 Jun, St-Pierre, patron saint of fishermen; grape picking festival, early Sep.
Walking La Promenade des Lombards: retracing historical episodes by the sea and up to the castle and cliffs.

CASTELLANE
Map ref 133 F6
Pop 1,500
Digne 54 km
Toulon 140 km
Marseille 164 km
Nîmes 252 km
Paris 812 km
🅵 route Nationale
☎ 92.83.61.14

Dominated by a huge limestone rock, this is a pretty little town and a lovely spot for a country holiday at the edge of one of the most famous natural spectacles in France, the **Gorges du Verdon**. Canoeing and even white-water rafting are available here, while walkers can choose from numerous routes to sample the scenery. Some of the routes are challenging, however, and suitable only for experienced walkers or those with guides. The nearby Lac de Castillon provides further watersports activities. The

Le Grand Jardin **
2 rue Pierre Eydin
☎ *42.01.70.10*

Camping
Les Cigales **
route de Marseille
☎ *42.01.07.34*
300 places Mar-Oct

Youth Hostel
Les Calanques
La Fontasse
☎ *42.01.02.72*

Restaurant
Presqu'île
quartier Port-Miou
route des Calanques
☎ *42.01.03.77*

Hotels
Nouvel Hôtel du Commerce ***
place Marcel Sauvaire
☎ *92.83.61.00*
(and restaurant)
Grand Hôtel du Levant **
place Marcel Sauvaire
☎ *92.83.60.05*
(and restaurant)

town itself has a few reminders of its long history, including traces of the 14th-century town wall and the church of St-Victor. The main activity here now is as a holiday resort between Provence and the mountains, deservedly popular with tourists who are happy to take away local produce such as lavender and honey.

There are many attractive villages nearby, also supporting holiday activities, amongst them **St-André-des-Alpes**.

Ma Petit Auberge **
place Marcel Sauvaire
☎ *92.83.62.06*
Du Roc **
place de l'Eglise
☎ *92.83.62.65*
(and restaurant)

Camping
International
route de Digne
☎ *92.83.70.67*
80 places Apr-Oct
Camp du Verdon
Domaine de la Salaou
☎ *92.83.61.29*
420 places May-Sep
La Belvédère ***
quartier Salaou
☎ *92.83.62.60*
40 places Jun-Sep
Le Frédéric Mistral **
12 avenue Frédéric Mistral
☎ *92.83.62.27*
60 places open all year

Restaurants
Auberge du Teillon
La Garde
☎ *92.83.60.88*
Le Grilladin
26 route de Grasse
☎ *92.83.72.04*

PARAGLIDING, CASTELLANE

Leisure
Aerial Sports *Paragliding* ☎ *92.89.11.30*
Cycling *cycles for hire from 19 avenue Frédéric Mistral* ☎ *92.83.68.33*
Fishing *Category 1 fishing in the Verdon river and lakes. Enquiries Moulin de la Salaou* ☎ *92.83.65.79*
Riding *Plan de la Palud* ☎ *92.83.63.94; Ranch des Pionniers* ☎ *92.77.38.30*
Rock Climbing *Club catering for various standards, enquire at Tourist Office.*
Skiing *Downhill or cross-country at Soleilhas-Vauplane. Enquiries*
☎ *92.31.57.29*
Tradition *Festival du Pétardier, 31 Jan, commemorating the end of the Huguenot siege in 1586: procession, music.*
Walking *Mountain guides, walking tours*
☎ *92.83.67.92 and Cabanon du Verdon*
☎ *92.77.38.58*
Watersports *White-water rafting bookable at AN Rafting, Moulin de la Salaou*
☎ *92.83.70.83; Verdon Raft*
☎ *92.83.72.12; Eaux Vives du Monde*
☎ *92.77.31.95; Castellane Canoe-kayak Club* ☎ *92.83.70.61*

CAVAILLON
Map ref 136 A1
Pop 20,000
Avignon 24 km
Nîmes 69 km
Marseille 78 km
Toulon 142 km
Paris 703 km
🛈 79, rue Saunerie
☎ 90.71.32.01.

The name of Cavaillon is familiar throughout France for its sweet, pink melons, and the town is an important market-gardening centre, its agricultural wealth derived from its setting in the rich Durance valley.
Reminders of its past can be seen in the small heavily ornamented Roman arch, and the very attractive church of St-Véran. This Romanesque former cathedral still has its 12th-century apse and tower, alongside the 14th-century cloister and decorative 17th-century chapels.
Cavaillon's museum provides a wide-ranging view of the past: the archeological museum has a collection of early remedies, while the former bakery of a prosperous 18th-century synagogue illustrates the region's traditional protection of Jewish communities.
For those with energy for the brisk climb up to the Chapelle St-Jacques perched above the town, the view over the Durance valley and surrounding hills is magnificent; and the chapel itself is simple but charming.

Leisure
Art Association Culturelle Provençal et Comtadine: art, music, dance, drama, folklore ☎ 90.78.18.63
Cycling Cycle track, Cavaillon-Cereste, approx 60 km.
Golf See Avignon and Aix-en-Provence.
Guided Tours Wed morning, Jul and Aug; depart from the Roman Arch.
Open-Air Theatre George Brassens, evening performances Jul and Aug.
Riding El Dorado Ranch, Les Taillades ☎ 90.71.03.04
Tradition Fair of St-Gilles, first Sun in Sep; fair of St-Véran, four days around 13 Nov; folklore displays, Feb, Jul, Aug; Grand Corso, Ascension Thurs, floats, folk dancing.

Hotels
Christel ***
quartier Boscodomini
☎ 90.71.07.79
(and restaurant)
Arilys **
175 avenue du Pont
☎ 90. 76.11.11
(and restaurant)
Parc **
place du Clos
☎ 90.71.57.78
Toppin **
70 cours Gambetta
☎ 90.71.30.42
(and restaurant)

Camping
Camping de la Durance ***
digue des Grands Jardins
☎ 90.71.11.78
150 places open all year

Restaurants
Prévot
353 avenue Verdun
☎ 90.71.32.43
Nicolet
13 place Gambetta
☎ 90.78.01.56
Fin de Siècle
46 place Clos
☎ 90.71.12.27
Au Bon Accueil
35 rue Emile Zola
☎ 90.78.23.46

CHATEAUNEUF-DU-PAPE
Map ref 129 E5
Pop 2,000
Avignon 16 km
Nîmes 56 km
Marseille 108 km
Toulon 172 km
Paris 704 km
🛈 place du Portail
☎ 90.83.71.08

Châteauneuf-du-Pape takes its name from its status as the summer residence of John XXII, a 13th-century Avignon pope, but is now best known for its famous wines. Much of the small medieval centre has been lost, but the early 14th-century papal palace has been restored, and wine-producing references can be seen everywhere: there is a museum of traditional vineyard tools, and cellars are open for tastings.
Geology is always the foundation of good wine and here the alluvial pebbles of the Rhône on the terraces absorb the sun's warmth and reflect it upwards onto the ripening grapes.

Leisure
Golf 18-hole course at Golf Grand Avignon, les Chênes Verts, B.P. 121, 84270 Vedène ☎ 90.31.49.94; 18-hole course at Golf Club de Châteaublanc, route de Châteaublanc, 84310 Morières-les-Avignon ☎ 90.33.39.08
Museum Musée du Vigneron, wine-producers' museum, 84110 Rasteau ☎ 90.83.71.79
Riding Trekking, La Rebousse, 84350

Hotels
Hostellerie Château des Fines Roches ****
(2km south on the D17, then private road)
☎ 90.83.70.23
(and restaurant)
Le Logis d'Arnavel ***
route de Roquemaure
☎ 90.83.73.22
(and restaurant)
La Garbure
3 rue Joseph-Ducos
☎ 90.83..73.22
(and restaurant)

Camping
Municipal Islon St-Luc **
☎ 90.83.76.77
90 places Apr-Sep

Restaurant
La Mule du Pape
2 rue de la République
☎ 90.83.79.22

HORSE RIDING, CHATEAUNEUF-DU-PAPE

Courthezon ☎ *90.70.88.42*
Tradition *Fête des Vins St-Marc in Apr;*
Fête de Carmentran, Mar-Apr; musical
evenings Jul-Aug.
Wine *Cellars open for visits, information*
from Tourist Office.

LA CIOTAT
Map ref 141 D5
Pop 31,000
Marseille 32 km
Toulon 42 km
Nîmes 148 km
Paris 800 km
🛈 boulevard
Anatole-France
☎ 42.08.43.80

La Ciotat's Roman origins lay in what is now the old port. Independent until 1429, it has developed upwards and outwards, becoming an important naval shipyard. Prosperity arrived in particular in 1580 when much of the Marseille ship-building industry moved here to escape an outbreak of plague.

The English blockade in the early 19th century was a setback, but La Ciotat is now a prosperous seaside resort full of holidaymakers in summer, and its harbour full of yachts. The modest housing of the shipyard workers contrasts with the palm trees and the luxury villas of wealthy visitors. Naval employment is declining and new outlets for ship and boat construction are being sought.

Hotels
Ciotat le Cap ***
corniche du Lioquet
☎ *43.83.90.30*
(and restaurant)
King ***
avenue de St-Jean
☎ *42.83.14.57*
(and restaurant)
Best Western Miramar ***
3 boulevard Beaurivage
☎ *42.83.09.54*

Camping
Belle Plage ***
14 avenue de Fonsainte
☎ *42.83.14.72*
30 places May-Sep

THE MISTRAL WIND

In these days of the T.G.V. high-speed trains, the Mistral can no longer compete with the French railways. But like the trains, the wind comes from the north and the Rhône valley lends it speed. The Mistral is linked with Provence for good or ill. According to a pre-Revolutionary saying "Parliament, the Mistral and the River Durance are the three scourges of Provence".

Blowing down towards the Mediterranean, its pell-mell gusts catch hats, umbrellas, clouds, frail little boats, and fans the flames through whole forests when they catch fire. It lends you wings if you are going in the same direction, but don't try to walk against it - you will get nowhere!

In any case, no-one tries to meet it head-on; the church bell-towers are made of wrought-iron so that the wind can blow straight through without destroying them. Or is this meant to tame its pride? In classical times it was granted divine status! Cypress trees, reed like, bend but do not break, and hedges are planted to shield fields and buildings. Terraces are constructed on south-facing façades, sheltered by the bulk of the house, and the tiles along the edge of the roof are cemented onto the outer walls in double or triple layers.

There are many stories and superstitions about the qualities of the Mistral. In Marsillargues it was once believed to be capable of rendering young girls pregnant. Another tells of its beneficial action in clearing the air, and in so doing to have blown away or diverted various epidemics. It is also said that if it does not rise during the night, the number of days for which it will blow will be a multiple of three.

The importance of the Mistral almost obliterates awareness of other winds which originate from all points of the compass. The gentle 'largade', the terrible Levanter which brings rain, the 'poument' from America and the Sirocco from the opposite shores of the Mediterranean laden with dust from the African deserts.

La Ciotat-Plage is a 3-km stretch of sea
front and big hotels, with fine beaches and
an enviable sunshine record. Along the
coast are the beautiful coves known as
Calanques, fine places for sailing and
swimming. The chapel of Notre-Dame-de-
la-Garde faces the sea - a shrine to protect
sailors.

Leisure
Boat Trips To l'Ile Verte, the calanque de
Figurilles, and the chapel of Notre-Dame-
de-la-Garde.
Golf See Aubagne.
Museum Shipping and crafts.

DIGNE-LES-BAINS

Map ref 133 D4
Pop 17,000
Marseille 144 km
Toulon 152 km
Cannes 154 km
Nîmes 197 km
Paris 758 km
🛈 le Rond-Point
☎ 92.31.42.73

Set in the mountainous pre-Alps in a sunny,
sheltered valley where the olive trees meet
the winter snows, Digne is well established
as a spa resort with fine modern buildings
for treating rheumatic and respiratory
ailments.
Lavender products are an important
element in Digne's economy, and fields of
lavender combine with the magnificent
mountain scenery to provide an attractive
background to the wide variety of sporting
activities available locally. Places to visit in
the town include the Fondation Alexander
David Neel, a unique centre of Tibetan
research, and La Réserve Géologique,
illustrating the geographical wealth of the
region.
On its strategic site on a main route to the
Alps, and lying on the *Route Napoléon*
used by the Emperor after his escape from
Elba, there is a real sense of moving away
from what one thinks of as typical Provence
country and into the realm of the
mountains.
The tourist train, Le Train des Pignes, runs
from Digne down through the beautiful
mountain valleys to Nice, and it is
frequently used by walkers to reach the
starting point for their expeditions. Track
renovation works start in 1991.

Leisure
Aerial sports Flying, parascending, para-
gliding, motorized hang-gliding: Sports
Aériens, A.A.H.P., 13 rue du Docteur
Romieu ☎ 92.32.25.32
Astronomy Courses offered by Plein Air
Nature, 42 boulevard Victor Hugo
☎ 92.31.51.09; information from
Observatoire du Centre National du
Recherche Scientifique, 04870 St-Michel-
l'Observatoire. (Observatory open to the
public).
Geology Centre St-Benoît ☎ 92.31.51.31
Golf 18-hole course, St-Pierre de Gaubert
☎ 92.32.38.38, also with tennis courts,
swimming pool and riding.
Leisure Centre Les Lacs de Ferréols,
route de Nice, swimming, boat hire,
climbing wall, ice-skating.
Riding Equitation L'Etrier, route des Clues
de Barles ☎ 92.32.12.96, instruction and
trekking.
Rock climbing Also mountaineering with
C.D. d'Escalade, 73 avenue Henri Jaubert
☎ 92.31.13.32

St-Jean ***
30 avenue de St-Jean
☎ 42.83.13.01
90 places Mar-Oct
Castel Joli **
route de Marseille
☎ 42.83.50.02
110 places Mar-Oct

Restaurant
Auberge Le Revestel
corniche du Liouquet
☎ 42.08.99.59

Hotels
Ermitage Napoléon ***
33 boulevard Gambetta
☎ 92.31.01.09
(and restaurant)
Le Grand Paris ***
19 boulevard Thiers
☎ 92.31.11.15
(and restaurant)
Hôtel Mistre ***
65 boulevard Gassendi
☎ 92.31.00.16
(and restaurant)
Central **
26 boulevard Gassendi
☎ 92.31.31.91
L'Aiglon **
1 rue de Provence
☎ 92.31.02.70
(and restaurant)
Le Coin Fleuri **
9 boulevard Victor Hugo
☎ 92.31.04.51
(and restaurant)

Camping
Les Eaux Chaudes ***
route des Thermes
☎ 92.32.31.04
90 places Apr-Oct
Camping le Bourg **
route de Barcelonette
☎ 92.31.04.87

Restaurant
l'Origan
6 rue Pied-de-Ville
☎ 92.31.62.13

THE HAUTE-PROVENCE GEOLOGICAL RESERVE

Lying between the Alps and Provence and established in 1984, the Haute-Provence geological reserve offers a glimpse of the earth's history during three hundred million years. The fossils and natural features visible in the reserve tell us much about the past.

The primary era is represented by vegetable deposits: encouraged by the warm damp climate, a vast tropical forest covered the region.

The fluctuating presence of the sea in the secondary era - it retreated for the last time in the tertiary period, with the appearance of the Alps - has left traces of contemporary marine fauna. There are ammonites (more than 500 fossils on a single 200 square-metre stone), belemnites, pentacrites, lamellibranchia, etc. The most impressive item is a Ichthyosaurus skeleton over 4 m in length - a reptile adapted to aquatic life. Discovered in 1979, it is displayed on the site where it was discovered, lying in a clear open-air structure which is unique in Europe. Apart from these marine fossils of the tertiary era there are also traces of footprints left by birds along the shore-line.

The features of the reserve clearly reveal the presence of the sea, and evidence of further geological activities of note are:

the fossil coral reef at St-Lions, thirty million years old which grew in the clear shallow waters;

the Digne overthrust - a range of mountain peaks consisting of the Cousson, the Siron, and the Blayeu, and the Barre des Doubes - which was the result of a colossal landslide four million years ago;

the Péroué cluses, the transverse valley formations at the time of the formation of the Pyrenees and the Alps;

the Verdaches cluses, cutting into the primary era outcrops;

the Chabrières cluses, where limestone strata from the upper Jurassic or secondary era have been pushed upright by the tectonic shifts.

Spa *Rheumatism/bone joint damage (Mar-Dec)* ☎ *92.31.06.68*
Tradition *International sculpture symposium, Jun; Songs of Provence and Summer Cinema festival, Jul; Tibetan festival, Jul; lavender festival, Aug.*
Walking *Information and maps for exploring on foot, cycle or horseback, from ADRI-CIMES, 42 boulevard Victor Hugo* ☎ *92.31.07.01; Plein Air Nature (same address)* ☎ *92.31.51.09; mountain walking guides: C.Thomas-Javid, 04460 Selonnet* ☎ *92.35.17.92*
Watersports *Swimming, white-water sports: Sports Nautiques and Eau Vive, 13 rue du Docteur Romieu* ☎ *92.32.25.32*

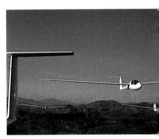
GLIDING, DIGNE

FONTAINE-DE-VAUCLUSE
Map ref 130 F2
Pop 600
Avignon 29 km
Nîmes 70 km
Marseille 94 km
Toulon 158 km
Paris 743 km
🏮 chemin de la Fontaine
☎ 90.20.32.22

This small village has become something of an international tourist attraction. It is beautifully located beneath the flanks of the plateau de Vaucluse and it has one of the most powerful springs in the world, gushing at a dramatic rate during high water periods out of a major subterranean river at the foot of a great cliff. The peacefulness of this place, and the racing green water cascading into waterfalls, overhung by leafy trees, once inspired the Italian poet Petrarch (1304-1374), and a museum in the town is devoted to him. The mysterious river and its underground course are the origins of the Norbert-Casteret speleological museum, and now provides the backdrop for elegant waterside restaurants and the sports of fishing and canoeing.

A short way downstream is the larger town of L'Isle-sur-Sorgue, with a series of small bridges across the river, and the occasional water mill. Other attractive villages to visit include Saumane-de-Vaucluse, with an imposing castle in an area well known for its truffles, and Le Thor

Hotels
Hôtel du Parc **
Les Bourgades
☎ *90.20.31.57*
(and restaurant)
Les Sources **
route de Cavaillon
☎ *90.20.31.84*
(and restaurant)
Hôtel de la Font de Laure
Plan de Saumane
☎ *90.20.31.49*

Camping
Municipal les Prés **
☎ *90.20.32.38*
100 places Feb-Nov
Municipal la Sorguette ***
route d'Apt
Isle-sur-Sorgue
☎ *90.38.05.71*
160 places Mar-Oct

FONTAINE-DE-VAUCLUSE

with its fine Romanesque church and
fortified chapel.

Leisure

Climbing Accompanied climbs in the
Dentelles de Montmirail. Short courses are
offered by the Monts du Vaucluse guides
and enquiries should be made at the
Tourist Office.

Golf See Avignon.

Museums Norbert-Casteret museum of
underground exploration; Petrarch
museum.

Riding Centre Equestre La Catherine,
chemin du Languien, 84800 Isle-sur-
Sorgue ☎ 90.38.16.13

Tradition Festival La Sorgue, Jul.

Watersports Canoeing with Sorgue-Kayak
Vert ☎ 90.20.35.44

FORCALQUIER
Map ref 131 E1
Pop 4,000
Aix-en-Provence
79 km
Marseille 109 km
Nîmes 147 km
Toulon 168 km
Paris 820 km
i place Bourget
☎ 92.75.10.02

The 'land of four queens' for this was the
home of the medieval Count Raimond of
Provence, each of whose four daughters
married a king.

Forcalquier is an old market town deep in
the heart of Provence, clinging to the
hillside of the farming uplands above the
River Durance, in an area of lavender,
thyme and tranquillity where the underlying
rocks are near the surface and the old
farms are built like small fortresses. The
simplicity of design of the Romanesque
church of Notre-Dame-de-Provence
accentuates its elegant Gothic porch, with,
in front, a pretty fountain and an orientation
table. Close by is the old Jewish quarter
and synagogue, and the museum, housed
in a particularly well-restored former
Franciscan convent in the midst of the old
streets, has an interesting collection that
includes archeology, local art, and
Provençal furniture.

The clarity of the atmosphere has always
attracted painters to the area, and was the
reason for the establishment of the Haute
Provence Observatory, 9 km to the west,

Restaurants

Hostellerie le Château
quartier Château Vieux
☎ 90.20.31.54

Philip
☎ 90.20.31.81

La Rascasse d'Argent
☎ 90.20.33.52

Hotels

Hostellerie des Deux Lions **
11 place du Bourguet
☎ 92.72.25.30
(and restaurant)

Grand Hôtel **
10 boulevard Latourette
☎ 92.75.00.35

Auberge Charembeau **
route de Niozelles
☎ 92.75.05.69
(and restaurant)

Camping

Camping St-Promasse **
route de Sigonce
☎ 92.75.27.94
66 places Apr-Sep

Restaurants

l'Atelier
3 rue Cordeliers
☎ 92.75.22.50

La Souste
1 boulevard de la République
☎ 92.75.05.82

THE OBSERVATORY OF HAUTE-PROVENCE

The clarity of St-Michel's air was the deciding factor which brought the astronomical observatory to this modest little village.

Created in 1936 by the newly-established C.N.R.S. (Centre National de la Recherche Scientifique; the national centre for scientific research), the Observatoire de Haute-Provence was in its day the most modern in France and successor to the late 19th-century establishments. It lies on a chalk plateau at a height of 650 m, some 2.5 km from the village and 9 km from Forcalquier.

The Observatory consists of thirteen domes with multiple instrumentation. The most important is the great telescope, the only one open to visitors. Brought into use in 1958, it is 1.93 m in diameter, weighs 1,200 kg and is equipped with the most up-to-date equipment (CDD camera, computer control and data acquisition, for the initiated).

The 1.52 m telescope, dating from 1969 is used essentially to measure the speed of star movements and their chemical atmospheric make-up.

The Observatory has a staff of about 100 plus, since 1986, seven astronomers working on a range of programmes - changes in stellar atmospheres, the evolution of the Seyfer galaxies and of quasars, the distance of supernovae; numerous French and foreign researchers come to the Observatory every year.

Visiting times: 2-4 each Wed; and, from Apr-Sep, the first Sun of each month at 9.30, except on public holidays. Groups are not accepted between 1 Jul and 31 Aug.

---

equipped with one of Europe's most powerful telescopes. Forcalquier is a good base for exploring the hill villages and valleys of the Lubéron and Mont Ventoux areas.

Leisure

Golf 18-hole course at Golf de Pierrevert, Domaine de la Grande Motte, 04860 Pierrevert ☎ 92.72.17.19: challenging course in typical Provençal scenery.

Guided Tours Organised by the Tourist Office, Wed and Sat mornings.

Museums Convent of the Visitation, archeology, regional art. Exhibitions on the history of Haute Provence: Alpes de Lumière, Prieurée de Salagon, Mane ☎ 92.75.19.93

Tradition Fête de St-Pancrace, mid May; Haute-Provence, Aug: Festival d'Eté du Théâtre de Haute-Provence ☎ 92.78.37.73

Walking Ramblers' Festival, May; information on exploring the countryside,

GORDES

Map ref 130 F2
Pop 1,600
Apt 29 km
Nîmes 81 km
Marseille 94 km
Toulon 159 km
Paris 754 km
🄸 place du Château
☎ 90.72.02.75

Gordes is one of Provence's most picturesque *villes perchées* or hilltop villages, its ancient houses of golden stone climbing up the escarpment round the massive Renaissance fortress and the little stone-paved lanes winding up and down the hillside. Sometimes it is difficult to see where the rock ends and the well-preserved houses begin, but in an interesting combination of the old and the modern, five of the castle's magnificent rooms are devoted to works by the 20th-century artist Vasarely.

Another style of building is visible in the neighbouring village of **Les Bories**: round dry-stone constructions whose history is uncertain, although they probably date from the 17th-19th centuries. Similar buildings exist elsewhere in France, in Ireland and in Greece.

Gordes is a good base from which to explore other attractive villages in the Lubéron National Park, such as **Roussillon**, built on a bright ochre outcrop of sand and rock, and **Lacoste**, ancestral home of the

Hotels

*Bastide de Gordes ★★★★
Le Village, rue de la Combe
☎ 90.72.12.12
(and restaurant)
Domaine de l'Enclos ★★★★
route de Sénanque
☎ 90.72.08.22
(and restaurant)
Hôtel la Gacholle ★★★
route de Murs
☎ 90.72.01.36
Hôtel le Gordos ★★★
quartier Escortiels
☎ 90.72.00.75
Hôtel la Mayanelle ★★★
route de la Combe
☎ 90.72.00.28
(and restaurant)*

Camping

*Les Sources ★★★
route de Murs
☎ 90.72.12.48
100 places Apr-Oct*

GORDES

Restaurants
Les Mas Tourteron
quartier St-Blaises,
Les Imberts
☎ *90.72.00.16*
Auberge les Bories
route de Sénanque
☎ *90.72.00.51*

Marquis de Sade, whose castle still watches over the village's steep little lanes and stone houses. In another valley lies the simple and beautiful 12th-century Cistercian abbey of **Sénanque**. Isolated between the steep hillsides and its lavender field, the abbey is still active as a religious foundation but is also open to the public.

Leisure

Art Vasarely Museum in the château, extensive op-art display set up by the artist himself ☎ 90.72.02.89

Golf See Avignon.

Riding Centre Equestre des Luquets ☎ 90.72.07.97

Tradition Horse fair, mid-Jul; International Festival of Music and Drama, first half of Aug.

GREOUX-LES-BAINS

Map ref 138 B2
Pop 1,600
Aix-en-Provence 48 km
Marseille 83 km
Toulon 99 km
Nîmes 156 km
Paris 800 km
𝐢 5 avenue des Marronniers
☎ 92.78.01.08

Europe's oldest spa town is surrounded by some of France's most attractive countryside for relaxing and enjoying outdoor sports of all kinds. Visitors seeking Gréoux's spa waters and tourists alike appreciate the ideal climate and the air scented with lavender and thyme. Built on the side of a rocky slope above the Verdon river with its famous gorges not far away and the River Durance also near, Gréoux is perfect as an excursion base, particularly for walkers and fishermen.

The town retains traces of its ramparts and a 12th-century gate. The Château des Templiers, surrounded by well-maintained old houses, is under restoration.

Hotels
La Crémaillère ***
route de Riez
quartier San Peyre
☎ *92.74.22.29*
(and restaurant)
Lou San Peyre ***
avenue des Thermes
☎ *92.78.01.14*
(and restaurant)
Villa Borghèse ***
avenue des Thermes
☎ *92.78.00.91*
(and restaurant)

THE VERDON GORGES

Hôtel des Alpes **
19 avenue des Alpes
☎ *92.74.24.24*
(and restaurant)

Camping
Les Cygnes ***
Domaine Paludette
☎ *92.78.08.08*
180 places Mar-Oct
La Pinède **
route de St-Pierre
☎ *92.78.05.47*
70 places Apr-Oct

Restaurants
Le Troubadour
1 rue du Puy
☎ *92.78.11.42*
Relais des Templiers
8 avenue des Alpes
☎ *92.78.00.24*

Leisure
Aerial Sports Gliding with the Association Aéronautique Verdon/Alpilles at Vinon-sur-Verdon aerodrome (8km).
Golf See Forcalquier.
Riding Centre Equestre Château Laval, route de Valensole ☎ 92.78.08.16; Centre Equestre du domaine d'Aurabelle ☎ 92.78.84.14
Spa Rheumatism/bone joint damage, arthritis ☎ 92.74.22.22
Tradition Festival, Jul, Château des Templiers: crafts; 'Les Oralies' story-telling; Festival d'Eté de Haute-Provence ☎ 92.78.37.73
Walking In the spectacular Verdon gorges and all areas round Gréoux. Guided walks, enquire at the Tourist Office.
Watersports Sailing on Lac d'Esparron.

SLIPPING OVER THE BORDER   *into Côte-d'Azur*

HYERES
Map ref 143 E4
Pop 45,000
Toulon 17 km
Marseille 80 km
Nîmes 201 km
Paris 950 km
🛈 Rotonde Jean Salusse
☎ 94.65.18.55

A busy sailing and watersports resort at the southernmost tip of the Côte d'Azur with a superb sunshine record. The Romans and Greeks knew of Hyères, and its prosperity is based on salt, fishing and agriculture. In the 15th century Hyères was more important than Toulon, and many Renaissance houses still survive in the old town. The church of St-Louis, restored and extended in the 19th century, retains its original 13th-century porch, and the Tour St Blaise, the Romanesque remainder of a

Hotels
Le Paris ***
20 avenue de Belgique
☎ *94.65.33.61*
Les Pins d'Argent
Port St-Pierre
☎ *94.57.63.60*
Le Ceinturon **
12 boulevard Front de Mer,
Ayguarde-Ceinturon
☎ *94.66.33.63*
(and restaurant)

Templar command post, contains a museum of Provençal traditions and crafts. The ruins of the castle, demolished during the Wars of Religion in the 16th century, dominate the hilltop above the steep narrow streets.

In the 19th century the town began its career as an internationally famous holiday resort. British visitors have always appreciated this coast and Queen Victoria was a visitor to the town during her regular trips to this area. The arrival of the railway encouraged the town's thriving trade in early vegetables and flowers for despatch to the rest of France, and the broad streets of the modern town are lined with palm

HYERES

Hôtel du Soleil **
2 rue Rempart
☎ *94.65.16.26*
Hôtel Ibiscus **
14 avenue 1ère Division
Brosset
☎ *94.65.47.48*
(and restaurant)
Mas du Langoustier ***
Ile de Porquerolles
☎ *94.58.30.09*
(and restaurant)
Le Manoir ***
Ile de Port-Cros
☎ *94.05.90.52*

Camping
Domaine du Ceinturon
No 3 ****
☎ *94.66.32.65*
260 places Mar-Sep
Camping Rebout Clos
Rose-Marie ****
Les Salins d'Hyères
☎ *94.66.41.21*
55 places open all year
Domaine du Ceinturon
No 2 ***
Les Pins Maritimes
☎ *94.66.39.66*
400 places Jun-Aug

Restaurant
La Vielle Auberge
St-Nicolas ***
RN 98, route de la Londe
quartier St-Nicolas
☎ *94.66.40.01*

trees which are grown here for export. Of the three islands opposite, the **Iles d'Hyères**, the biggest is **Porquerolles**, noted for its fine beaches. The other two are **Ile du Levant**, a naturist centre, and **Port Cros**, a National Park with severe restrictions on camping and lighting fires, and with some unique flora and fauna. Ferries run from the modern beach resort of Hyères-Plage below the town, and from the Tour Fondue at **Giens**, the adjoining salt-producing peninsula.

Leisure
Boat Trips To the Iles d'Hyères from La Tour Fondue, Giens ☎ *94.58.21.81; from Port d'Hyères* ☎ *94.57.44.07*
Cycling Cycles can be hired from the SNCF station.
Golf 18-hole course at Golf de Valcros, Hyères, 83250 La Londe les Maures
☎ *94.66.81.02*
Riding Relais Equestre de la Ferme
☎ *94.66.41.78 and Centre Equestre St-Georges, Domaine de la Bravette*
☎ *94.57.24.00*
Tradition Festival Provençal
☎ *94.65.22.72*

ISTRES
Map ref 140 A1
Pop 30,000
Marseille 54 km
Nîmes 79 km
Toulon 115 km
Paris 787 km
🏛 30, allées Jean-Jaurès
☎ 42.55.51.16

Istres is set on a rocky spur between the large shallow Etang de Berre and the Crau, the flat fertile plain stretching west to the Rhône. In the old town plane trees replace the medieval walls and narrow lanes and steps lead up the hill, past fine 17th- and 18th-century houses with magnificent porches. From the fortified church with its 16th-century façade the view includes old tile rooftops and the small Etang d'Olivier below.
Reminders of Istres's most distant past can be seen in the Museum of Vieil Istres. Situated within a 17th-century house, on display are the many Greek amphorae and

Hotels
Le Mirage ***
avenue des Anciens Combattants
☎ *42.56.02.26*
Aystria Tartugues **
chemin de Tartugues
☎ *42.56.44.55*
Des Baumes **
boulevard de Vauranne
☎ *42.55.02.63*
(and restaurant)
Le Castellan **
place Ste-Catherine
☎ *42.55.13.09*

ISTRES

dolae (containers used for transporting food supplies) which were discovered during underwater archeological searches at **Fos**.
The 20th century is represented by the airfield near by, for Istres has been involved with flying since 1917. The base is now used for flight testing of new aircraft.
Leisure
Tradition Jousting and Provençal tradition fair, Jul; shepherds' festival, with 2,000 sheep in the streets, Dec.

Camping
Vitou ***
route de St-Chamas l'Estagel
☎ *42.56.51.57*

Restaurants
St-Martin
Port des Heures Claires
☎ *42.56.07.12*
Mazet de Pepi
ruen Baumes
☎ *42.55.42.43*

Hotels
Hôtel les Quintrands **
route de Sisteron
☎ *92.72.08.86*
(and restaurant)
Hôtel le Campanile **
route de Sisteron
☎ *92.87.59.00*
(and restaurant)
Hôtel François 1er **
18 rue Guilhempierre
☎ *92.72.07.99*

Camping
Camping Les Ubacs ***
avenue de la Repasse
☎ *92.72.28.08*
110 places Apr-Oct

MANOSQUE
Map ref 138 A1
Pop 19,000
Forcalquier 20 km
Marseille 85 km
Toulon 147 km
Nîmes 159 km
Paris 845 km
🏛 place Dr P.-Joubert
☎ 92.72.16.00

Manosque is strategically placed beside the River Durance, an important regional centre for agriculture and hydro-electric energy. It is also a very attractive town, set on a rounded hill and still retaining its fountains and twisting medieval streets of old stone houses with sandy-pink tiled roofs and impressive doorways and arcades. The Provençal writer Jean Giono, who was born here and who wrote frequently about its charms, said that "Manosque's true wealth is its beauty." The Porte Saunerie, once the southern entrance to the town, is a magnificent arched tower, while the Porte Soubeyran, its northern equivalent, is similar but with an iron belfry. The church of St-Sauveur, Romanesque in origin, is simple and typically Provençal. The clear air of Provence was responsible for the siting of Europe's largest astrophysical observatory in this region,

16km from Manosque. This modern scientific centre contrasts with the many well-preserved villages all around, particularly in the beautiful Lubéron National Park, a wonderful and unspoilt region for outdoor activities.

Leisure
Astronomy *Information from Observatoire du Centre National de Recherche Scientifique, 04870 St-Michel l'Observatoire (observatory open to the public).*
Golf *See Forcalquier.*
Kite Club *Cerf-Volant Club de France, Lotissement Eau Vive, rue Temple, 04100 Manosque* ☎ *92.78.02.94*
Riding *Centre Equestre le Pilon, Quartier des Naïsses, 04100 Manosque* ☎ *92.72.06.29*
Walking *Accompanied two- to nine-day walks, in the footsteps of Jean Giono in the Lubéron National Park or Gorges du Verdon areas with Plein-Air Nature, 42 boulevard Victor Hugo, 04000 Digne* ☎ *93.31.51.09*

MARSEILLE
Map ref 141 C4
Pop 880,000
Toulon 67 km
Nîmes 118 km
Paris 813 km
🛈 4 la Canebière
☎ 91.54.91.11
🛈 gare St-Charles
☎ 91.50.59.18

After 2,600 years of uninterrupted activity, Marseille has many reminders of its varied past. Founded by the Greeks, it has always been an active port, and when much of the old quarter was destroyed in 1943 parts of the Roman docks emerged. It is now the largest commercial port in the Mediterranean, and France's second city.

'La Canebière', its famous avenue of shops, hotels, restaurants and offices, leads down to the Vieux Port, its quays crowded with fishing and pleasure craft. Leading off the Canebière is the quarter of the cours Belsunce and the rue d'Aix, a maze of casbah-type stalls and shops, for the city has always been the focus of attraction for trade and visitors from Mediterranean, African and Far Eastern countries.

NOTRE-DAME-DE-LA-GARDE, MARSEILLE

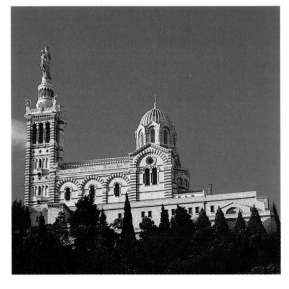

Youth Hostel
parc de la Rochette
☎ *92.87.57.44*

Restaurants
Hostellerie de la Fuste
La Fuste, Valensole
☎ *92.72.05.95*
André
21 bis, place Terreau
☎ *92.72.03.09*

Hotels
Sofitel Marseille Vieux Port ★★★★
36 boulevard Charles Livon
☎ *91.52.90.19*
(and restaurant)
Concorde Prado ★★★★
11 avenue de Mazaragues
☎ *91.76.51.11*
(and restaurant)
Pullman Beauvau ★★★★
4 rue Beauvau
☎ *91.54.91.00*
Le Petit Nice ★★★★
17 rue des Braves
☎ *91.59.25.92*
(and restaurant)
Altéa ★★★
1 rue Neuve St-Martin
☎ *91.39.20.00*
(and restaurant)
Castellane ★★★
31 rue de Rouet
☎ *91.79.27.54*
Concorde Palm Beach ★★★
2 promenade Georges Pompidou
☎ *91.76.20.00*
(and restaurant)
Européen ★★
115 rue Paradis
☎ *91.37.77.20*

Camping
Municipal Bonneveine ★★★★
187 Clot-Bey
☎ *91.73.26.99*
160 places Jun-Sep
Les Vagues ★★
52 avenue de Bonneveine
☎ *91.73.76.30*
120 places Jun-Sep

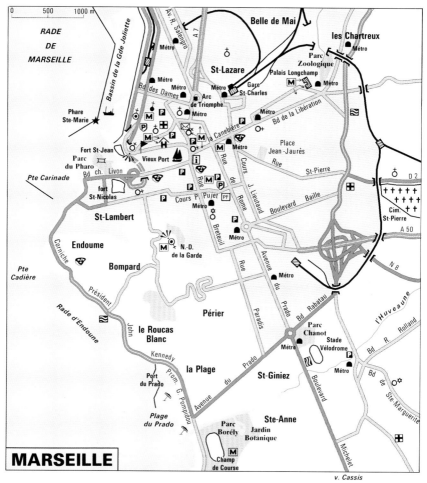

MARSEILLE

v. Cassis

The old cathedral has been sympatheti-
cally restored and is considered one of
Provence's finest Romanesque churches,
while the church of Notre-Dame-de-la-
Garde, watching over the old harbour, is a
worthy place of pilgrimage and a
magnificent viewpoint over the city and
surrounding landscape.
Marseille has a number of interesting
museums, and one of the city's most
striking elements is Le Corbusier's
residential complex, the 'Cité Radieuse' an
avant-garde experiment in architectural
design (1952). Offshore lies the Château
d'If, originally a prison and later the setting
for Alexandre Dumas's *Count of Monte
Cristo*. Boat trips leave from the old port for
a round trip of great interest, while drives
along the corniche road will reward you
with fine sandy beaches.

Leisure

Art The Musée des Beaux Arts in the
Longchamp Palace has works by Rubens,
David, Ingres, Corot and Watteau
☎ 91.62.21.17

Boat Trips To the Château d'If, the Iles du
Frioul, and the Calanques between
Marseille and Cassis. GACM, quai des
Belges ☎ 91.55.50.09 sail regularly to
Corsica and North Africa.

Youth Hostels

Château de Bois-Luzy
avenue de Bois-Luzy
☎ *91.49.06.18*
47 avenue J. Vidal
☎ *91.73.21.81*

Restaurants

Jambon de Parme
67 rue La Palud
☎ *91.54.37.01*
Au Pescadou
19 place Castellane
☎ *91.78.36.01*
Calypso
3 rue des Catalans
☎ *91.52.64.00*
Chez Fonfon
140 vallon des Auffes
☎ *91.52.14.38*
Michel
6 rue des Catalans
☎ *91.52.30.63*
Le Béarnais
16 rue St-Torrents
☎ *91.37.01.96*

Golf Golf d'Allauch, route des 4 Saisons,
13190 Allauch ☎ 91.05.20.60: 18-hole Golf
Country Club de la Salette, Impasse des
Vaudrans, La Valentine, 13011 Marseille
☎ 91.27.12.16; 18-hole golf d'Aix-
Marseille, Domaine de Riquetti, 13290 Les
Milles ☎ 42.24.20.21; Golf de Cabriès,
13480 Cabriès.
Guided Tours City tour and guide:
Histobus, l'Espace infos ☎ 91.91.92.10
Museums Musée Grobet-Labadie, iron
work, musical instruments and furniture
☎ 91.62.21.82; Musée Cantini, pottery
and contemporary art ☎ 91.54.77.75;
Musée Borely displays regional
archeology and drawings; Musée du
Vieux-Marseille ☎ 91.55.10.19; Musée
d'Histoire ☎ 91.90.42.22; Musée des
Docks Romains, the only open-air
museum in the region: Roman harbour
☎ 91.56.28.38
Riding Centre Equestre Sportif, chemin de
la Bédoule, Carnoux-en-Provence
☎ 42.84.37.80
Sailing Centre Municipal de Voile,
promenade de la Plage ☎ 91.76.31.60;
Association pour la promotion des
Multicoques, 45 boulevard du Point-de-Vue
☎ 91.96.05.65
Spa Nearby at Camoins-les-Bains,
respiratory/lymphatic disorders (1 Mar-15
Dec) ☎ 91.43.02.50
Tradition International Choral Festival, Jun;
Parc Borély, largest pétanque competition
in the world, 15-18 Jul; pilgrimage to Notre-
Dame-de-la-Garde, 8 Sep; Santons fair,
two weeks in Nov.

MOUSTIERS POTTERY

In the 17th century Moustiers-Ste-Marie became the Provençal capital of the art of *faïence*, earthenware pottery decorated with enamel and glaze. There are two reasons for the growth of this craft in this
particular commune: first, the malleable qualities of the local clay, and secondly, the enthusiasm for
earthenware pottery at the court of the Kings of France, which provided a steady market.

The most famous earthenware of the period was produced by Pierre Clarisay, working with the artist
Viry. Inspired by Italian tradition, his work was decorated with historical or mythological hunting scenes
in blue cameo.

Polychrome decoration was introduced in 1738
by Joseph Olerys. Working with Jean-Baptiste
Laugier he produced pottery embellished with
rocaille, enamel-based motifs of garlands and
medallions, grotesque figures or solanum flowers.
Le Berain was another designer who inspired the
Moustiers craftsmen.

By the end of the 18th century, however, *faïence*
was losing its high prestige, and although the
workshops were still turning it out, sales were
limited during the 19th century to Provence alone.
It was during this period that the style and range
known so well in modern times was developed.
The classic "Moustiers" style consists of plant
motifs and scenes with animals, with flowing
curves, and with blue, yellow and olive green the
dominant colours.

Although the growth of modern tourism has
emphasized the decorative aspects of Moustiers
pottery, it is worth remembering that originally and
until comparatively recently it was used for
everyday household purposes in Provence.

MOUSTIERS FAIENCE

MARTIGUES
Map ref 140 B1
Pop 42,000
Aix-en-Provence
45 km
Marseille 27 km
Nîmes 69 km
Toulon 142 km
Paris 760 km
🛈 quai P.-Doumer
☎ 42.80.30.72

What was originally a Roman port and then a small fishing village by the Etang de Berre, still retains its old quarters and the picturesque charm which beguiled Corot and other 19th-century artists.

Despite the town's recent and considerable industrial expansion, the canals dividing the town into three sections (once independent towns) still reflect the elegant façades of its old houses, and the restored ancient centre is an attractive reminder of old-style Provençal life.

Martigues is sometimes known as the "the Venice of Provence" with its little islets and many branching canals. The former Custom House contains some fine archeological and ethnological collections and some interesting 19th-century Provençal art.

Nearby **Port-de-Bouc** has a copy of the bridge made famous by Van Gogh in his painting *Pont de Langlois* (the original was pulled down in 1926) and **Châteauneuf-les-Martigues** is a picturesque village with a Romanesque chapel and archeological museum.

Leisure
Tradition *Jousting festival, first Sun in Jul; international folk festival, Châteauneuf-les-Martigues, Aug; Moulinet d'Or, musical evenings, Aug.*

Hotels
St Roch ***
ancienne route de Port-de-Bouc
☎ *42.80.19.73*
(and restaurant)
Eden ***
boulevard Emile Zola
☎ *42.07.36.37*
(and restaurant)
Fimotel **
Zone industrielle sud
☎ *42.81.84.94*
(and restaurant)
Gril Campanile **
2 boulevard de Tholon
☎ *42.80.14.00*
(and restaurant)
Le Lido **
cours du 4 septembre
☎ *42.07.00.32*
(and restaurant)

Camping
L'Arquet Municipal ***
chemin de la Batterie
☎ *42.42.81.00*
400 places Apr-Sep

MOUSTIERS-STE-MARIE
Map ref 138 A4
Pop 500
Castellane 54 km
Marseille 119 km
Toulon 127 km
Nîmes 192 km
Paris 892 km
🛈 Syndicat d'Initiative
☎ 92.74.67.84

Moustiers's dramatic setting, nestled beneath a deep cleft at the entrance to the great gorges of the River Verdon, is in sharp contrast with the pure air which carries with it the scent of thyme and lavender, and the peaceful silence of the mountains.

The old town is an attractive mix of lanes and little squares surrounded by arcades and magnificent houses, many with corbelled façades. The church of Notre-Dame combines Provençal Romanesque and Gothic styles with evidence of Lombard influence and dates from the 12th-16th centuries.

The two rocky peaks of Moustiers are linked by a chain slung across the gorge, which was probably first positioned as the result of a crusader's vow. The original, reportedly made of silver, was stolen during the Wars of Religion in the 16th century.

Moustiers has an ancient china-manufacturing tradition, the famous *faïences de Moustiers*, which reached its peak in the 17th and 18th centuries. It is a craft which has now been revived and is once again bringing prosperity, with the renewed interest of tourists and collectors alike.

Attractive walks and drives along the **Gorges du Verdon** start from Moustiers; the twists and cliffs of this outstandingly impressive river canyon providing a succession of magnificent views while the spreading waters of the Ste-Croix lake situatedbetween Moustiers and the Ste-Croix dam offer the tourist every kind of watersport.

Hotels
Le Belvédère **
☎ *92.74.66.04*
(and restaurant)
La Bonne Auberge **
route de Castellane
☎ *92.74.66.18*
(and restaurant)
Le Colombier **
quartier St-Michel
☎ *92.74.66.02.*

Camping
Camping St-Jean ***
quartier St-Jean
☎ *92.74.66.85*
110 places Apr-Sep
Camping le Vieux Colombier ***
quartier St-Michel
☎ *92.74.61.89*
70 places Easter-Sep
Camping St-Clair **
☎ *92.74.67.15*
220 places Apr-Sep
Camping Le Petit Lac **
☎ *92.74.67.11*
100 places Apr-Sep

Restaurants
Les Santons
place de l'Eglise
☎ *92.74.66.48*
La Ferme Rose
quartier Melen
☎ *92.74.69.47*

Leisure
Aerial Sports Hang-gliding, ultra-light and
paragliding ☎ 92.74.62.05
Climbing Falaise de l'Ourbes, enquire at
the Tourist Office or ☎ 92.31.13.32
Riding Ranche Reata ☎ 92.74.60.14
Tradition Festival and pilgrimage to the
chapel of Notre-Dame-de-Beauvoir, 8 Sep.
Walking For further information concerning
accompanied walks and climbs in the
Verdon gorges contact the Tourist Office
☎ 92.74.67.84
Watersports Sailing, sailboard, canoe-
kayak and rafting ☎ 92.74.60.71

NANS-LES-PINS
Map ref 138 E1
Pop 1,300
Marseille 40 km
Toulon 72 km
Nîmes 164 km
Paris 800 km
🛈 rue Georges-
Clémenceau
☎ 94.78.95.91

A pretty village and summer holiday resort
lying in the foothills of the Ste-Baume
massif, Nans-les-Pins is surrounded by
vineyards and pine trees. Principal sites to
visit here are the château ruins and, thirty
minutes walk away, the intermittent spring
known as the "Grande Foux". Fed by
waters filtering underground, the spring
gushes out of a deep cave.
From the 17th to the 19th centuries, one of
the Sainte-Baume hills' main products was
ice, with up to 3,000 tonnes being
produced from the ice-houses of Fontrège
each summer. Modern visitors may enjoy
thinking of this pre-refrigeration industry as
they explore the beauties of the area in
high summer!
This is an area for outdoor exploration and
sport, with footpaths crossing the almost
unpopulated hillsides and leading up to the
magnificent viewpoint of St-Pilon, a few
kilometres to the south of Nans-les-Pins.
Much of the massif is almost bare rock
covered with sparse heathland. The upland
region, however, has a protected forest
with a wide variety of trees and wild
flowers, many of them very rare.
Leisure
Golf See Maximin-la-Ste-Baume.

Hotels
Domaine de Châteauneuf ****
☎ 94.78.90.06
(and restaurant)
La Broche Provençale **
route de Ste-Baume
☎ 94.78.90.38
(and restaurant)

SLIPPING OVER THE BORDER   *into Languedoc-Roussillon*

NIMES
Map ref 134 A2
Pop 130,000
Avignon 42 km
Marseille 118 km
Toulon 186 km
Paris 740 km
🛈 6 rue Auguste
☎ 66.67.29.11

Nîmes spans the whole of French history.
The crocodile on the city's coat of arms
refers to the Emperor Augustus, victor
along the Nile, who founded the Roman
city. Surviving Roman buildings include a
perfect temple and the world's best-
preserved Roman arena.
There have been many wars in Nîmes's
history: the Visigoths drove out the
Romans, Simon de Montfort's crusaders
defeated the Albigensian heretics or
Cathars, and the city was at the centre of
Protestant resistance in the 16th and 17th
centuries.
Nîmes today is a prosperous city with a
well-preserved ancient heart, much of it
pleasantly pedestrianized.
A leader in the wool and silk industries,
Nîmes supposedly supplied the denim
material (*de Nîmes*) to make the original
blue jeans.
The impressive Roman temple known as

Hotels
Imperator Concorde ***
place A.-Briand
☎ 66.21.90.30
(and restaurant)
Louvre ***
2 square de la Couranne
☎ 66.67.22.75
(and restaurant)
Mercure ***
chemin de l'Hostellerie
parc hôtelier
Ville active
☎ 66.84.14.55
(and restaurant)
Majestic **
10 rue Pradier
☎ 66.29.24.14
De Milan **
17 avenue Feuchères
☎ 66.29.29.90

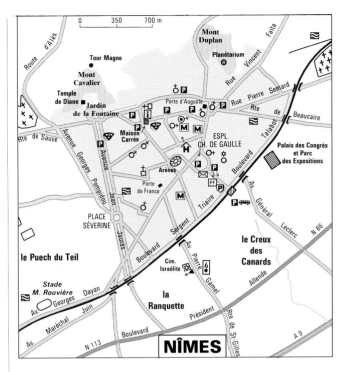

the Maison Carré is today a museum of local antiquities, and the great Roman arena, used as a fortress and then as living quarters in the Middle Ages, now seats audiences of 16,000 for various traditional types of bullfighting.

Other sites to visit include the Fountain Gardens designed by Le Nôtre on the site of the ancient Roman baths, and the vaulted temple of Diana.

A few kilometres away the beautiful and technically impressive three-tiered Pont-du-Gard is another reminder of the Roman genius for building. Part of the 50km aqueduct that supplied Nîmes with water for many centuries, it is deservedly popular with tourists.

Leisure

Carriage Tours Horse-drawn city sightseeing; depart from the place des Arènes.

Cycle Hire Bicycles can be hired from the SNCF station.

Golf Varied and very attractive 18-hole course at Golf de Nîmes Campagne, route de Saint-Gilles, 30000 Nîmes ☎ 66.70.17.37; 18-hole course at Golf Nîmes Vacquerolles ☎ 66.23.33.33

Museums Musée des Beaux Arts, rue Cité Foulc ☎ 66.67.38.21; Nimagine, Salon of Contemporary Art, two weeks in Nov; Natural History Museum in boulevard Amiral Courbet ☎ 66.67.39.14; antiquities museum, Maison Carré ☎ 66.67.25.57; and old Nîmes museum of local art and history, Palais de l'Ancien Evêché ☎ 66.36.00.64

Riding and Walking Enquire at the Tourist Office.

Tradition Feria de Pentecôte, Whit week,

Carrière **
6 rue Grizot
☎ 66.67.24.89
(and restaurant)

Camping

Municipal de la Bastide ***
route de Générac
☎ 66.38.09.21
230 places open all year

Youth Hostel

chemin de la Cigale
☎ 66.23.25.04

Restaurants

Alexandre
Garons
☎ 66.70.08.99
Au Cocotier
15 rue Pierre Sémand
☎ 66.67.83.29
Mas des Abeilles
route de St-Gilles
☎ 66.38.28.57

arena sports, Flamenco festival, street displays. Feria des Vendanges, grape-harvest, folk dancing, arena sports, last weekend in Sep.

ORANGE
Map ref 129 D5
Pop 27,000
Avignon 28 km
Nîmes 59 km
Marseille 122 km
Toulon 187 km
Paris 691 km
i cours Aristide-Briand
☎ 90.34.70.88

Owned by the Dutch Princes of Orange between the 16th and 18th centuries, this southern French town of Roman origin has seen its name appear all over the world. Its Roman past is still vividly evident in two of France's most impressive surviving monuments; the spectacular Roman theatre built in the first century AD, with seating for 10,000 spectators, and the highly decorated Triumphal Arch. The great back wall of the theatre is the only one in the world to have survived complete from ancient times, and the excellent accoustics of the amphitheatre are demonstrated in July and August each year during the 'Chorégies', operatic and choral performances which attract international audiences. The Triumphal Arch, lying on the track of the Via Agrippa running from Lyon to Arles, is particularly well preserved and of unusual design with scenes depicting the victories of Roman armies in Gaul.

The streets and houses of the old town are attractively Provençal in style, with squares planted with plane trees for deep shade. There are also the old churches of Notre-Dame-de-Nazareth and St-Florent to explore, representing between them the 12th and 13th centuries.

Hotels
Altéa ***
route de Caderousse
☎ 90.34.24.10
(and restaurant)
Arène ***
place de Langes
☎ 90.34.10.95
Louvre et Terminus ***
89 avenue Frédéric Mistral
☎ 90.34.10.08
(and restaurant)
Boscotel **
764 avenue Général-de-Gaulle
☎ 90.34.47.50
(and restaurant)
Hôtel Cigaloun **
4 rue Caristie
☎ 90.34.10.07

Camping
Le Jonquier ***
rue Alexis Carrel
☎ 90.34.19.83
150 places Mar-Oct
Municipal **
Colline St-Eutrope
☎ 90.34.09.22
240 places Mar-Oct

Restaurants
Le Pigraillet
chemin Colline St-Eutrope
☎ 90.34.44.25
Le Provençal
27 rue de la République
☎ 90.34.01.89
Parvis
3 cours Pourtoules
☎ 90.34.82.00
Le Barque aux Romarins
Ferme auberge (4 km south)
quartier de Bois Feuillet
☎ 90.34.55.96

HORSE RIDING, ORANGE

Leisure
Golf 9-hole course at Golf du Moulin, route de Camaret ☎ 90.34.34.04
Riding Trekking and lessons, Ecole d'Equitation, route du Parc ☎ 90.51.63.85
Tradition Chorégies, international music festival, Jul-Aug ☎ 90.51.83.83; film festival, last week in Nov.
Wine Wine fair, the Côtes du Rhône wines, Jan; wine tasting, prizewinners of the Jan fair in the Roman theatre, Jul-Aug.

THE PROVENCAL LANGUAGE

With his talents as a writer Frédéric Mistral brought a new cultural breath of life to Provençal. He described his linguistic heritage:

"Born in Nîmes, into an ultra-bourgeois trading family, I grew up amid scorn and disdain for what my parents called the local patois and which I must, under threat of the severest punishment, leave to servants, workmen, common people and the streets. And the more severely I was forbidden to like it, the more I loved this patois of the streets and countryside. As a captive schoolboy I found all these vivid sounds sparkling in my melancholy spirit: they seemed to my yearnings like those sharp and bitingly acid little red fruits - jujubes, sorb-apples, medlars - spread out in abundance among the strings of onions and jumbal biscuits under the plane trees by the tower, at St-Michel's fair".

Derived from Latin, the Provençal language belongs to the extended family of Occitan tongues which were spoken in southern France until the early 20th century. Used for both legal and literary purposes, it acquired what was virtually its final definitive form by the 10th century.

As a legal language, it established the rules used in the application of Roman Law texts; this contrasts with the North of France, where custom alone had the force of law until the unifying legislation introduced after the French Revolution.

As a literary tongue Provençal was the troubadours' means of expression: nobles - the most famous among them being Guillaume IX, Duke of Aquitaine - and commoners alike wrote about "Courtly love", the crusades, devotion to the saints - and also satires, in the form of songs.

In the 16th century, during the reign of François I, Provençal lost its status as the language of administration and entered a long dormant period as a literary tongue, although it remained a lively spoken language. There were some remarkable exceptions to this general rule: it was used by the 16th-century astrologer Michel de Nostre-Dame - known as Nostradamus - author of the famous prophecies, and others, including Bellaud de la Bellaudière and Michel Tron.

In the 19th century the Romantic movement brought the Middle Ages and the troubadours back into fashion. This was a time of literary revival, seen in the work of the Marseille writer Victor Gelu, to a greater extent with Mistral's work *Mireille* (1859) and, in 1854, the "Félibrige". The influence of this movement, which brought together writers of the Provençal language, was felt in art and literature until the 1940s.

The spread of compulsory education from the late 19th century onwards meant that everyone was required to learn French, and Provençal was reduced to the level of a simple folk dialect used only by the old.

Some town councils, including notably Aix-en-Provence, put up plaques indicating the former street names and there are attempts to keep the language alive, occasionally putting it in the broader framework of claims of regional identity.

The most obvious trace of Provence's linguistic past can be observed nowadays in the sing-song accent of southern French: beware of imitating it, however, the people of Provence will not appreciate your efforts!

ST-MAXIMIN-LA-STE-BAUME

Map ref 138 E2
Pop 5,000
Aix-en-Provence
36 km
Marseille 50 km
Toulon 55 km
Nîmes 164 km
Paris 840 km
🛈 Hôtel de Ville
☎ 94.78.00.09

The most important building in St-Maximin-la-Ste-Baume is its 13th-century church established in honour of St-Maximin and Ste-Marie Madeleine, both of whom are said to have been buried here. According to legend, Ste-Marie Madeleine spent thirty years living as a penitent in her Ste-Baume grotto and was transported to this spot by angels as she was dying. St-Maximin was the first Bishop of Aix-en-Provence, and died a martyr.

The little houses are set around picturesque squares and fountains and press closely round the great Gothic church which is built in the northern style, making it unique in Provence. The cloisters are beautiful, full of light and freshness and there is plenty of music to be heard here for the 18th-century organ has survived intact and concerts of French music are given every summer.

Originally fortified, the town lies on the old Roman road, the Via Aurelia, and grew up around the church as ever increasing numbers of pilgrims visited the tombs. This delightful little town lies on the edge of a broad plain near the forest-covered Ste-Baume massif.

Hotels
Hôtel de France **
1 avenue Albert 1er
☎ *94.78.00.14*
(and restaurant)
Hôtel Plaisance **
20 place Malherbe
☎ *94.78.16.74*

Camping
Camping le Provençal ***
route de Mazaugues
☎ *94.78.16.97*
100 places Apr-Oct

Restaurant
Chez Nous
3 boulevard J.-Jaurès
☎ *94.78.02.57*

Leisure
Golf 18-hole private course at Golf de la Ste-Baume, 83860 Nans-les-Pins
☎ *94.78.60.12, set in a long narrrow valley with a river running through it; Golf de Barbaroux, 83180 Brignolles*
☎ *94.59.07.43*
Tradition *Flower festival, late Apr; bric-à-brac, early Jul; Marie-Madeleine, crafts, late Jul; music, Jun-Aug.*

ST-REMY-DE-PROVENCE
Map ref 135 B5
Pop 9,000
Arles 28 km
Nîmes 41 km
Marseille 86 km
Toulon 150 km
Paris 745 km
ℹ place Jean-Jaurès
☎ 90.92.05.22

In the heart of the Provençal fruit-growing area, St-Rémy lies next to some spectacular Roman ruins known as Les Antiques which consist of the excavated site of Glanum, the ruins of a mausoleum and a commemorative arch celebrating the Roman conquest of Gaul.
One of the town's most interesting medieval buildings is the former monastery of St-Paul-de-Mausole, an asylum since the days of the French Revolution and where, in the late 19th century, Vincent Van Gogh spent the last year of his life. Quite apart from this artistic connection, the monastery cloisters are worth viewing in their own right. Van Gogh painted some of his most famous works in the St-Rémy area, drawn to the place by the rare quality of the light and the brilliant Provençal colouring of the surrounding countryside.
The great Provençal poet Frédéric Mistral was born near St-Rémy at **Maillane** in 1830, and the house built for him there is now a museum.
There are magnificent walks amid thyme and lavender along the footpaths of the **Alpilles** massif, for this is an area of many aromatic plants and flowers which can be discovered on foot, horseback or bicycle. There is also gliding and fishing and, for the benefit of the visitor, cockade racing and the traditional Release of the Bulls.

LES ANTIQUES, ST-REMY-DE-PROVENCE

Hotels
Château des Alpilles ****
RD 31
☎ *90.92.03.33*
Les Antiques ***
15 avenue Pasteur
☎ *90.92.03.02*
Le Vallon de Valruges ****
chemin de Canto-Cigalo
☎ *90.92.04.40*
(and restaurant)
Le Castelet des Alpilles ***
6 place Mireille
☎ *90.92.07.21*
(and restaurant)
Le Mas des Carassins ***
1 chemin Gaulois
☎ *90.92.15.48*
Hôtel des Arts **
30 boulevard Victor Hugo
☎ *90.92.08.50*
(and restaurant)

Camping
Mas de Nicolas ****
avenue Théodore Aubanel
☎ *90.92.27.05*
140 places Mar-Oct
Pégomas ***
route de Noves
☎ *90.92.01.21*
105 places Mar-Oct
Montplaisir **
chemin Montplaisir
☎ *90.92.22.70*
90 places Mar-Nov

Restaurants
Le Jardin de Frédéric
8 boulevard Gambetta
☎ *90.92.27.76*
Marceau
13 boulevard Marceau
☎ *90.92.37.11*
Le Coupe-Chou
Verquiers, St-Andiol
☎ *90.95.18.55*
La Gousse d'Ail
25 rue Carnot
☎ *90.92.16.87*

GLANUM RUINS, ST-REMY-DE-PROVENCE

Leisure
Cycling *Cycles for hire locally at Location Florelia* ☎ *90.92.10.88*
Golf *See Les Baux-de-Provence.*
Museum *Frédéric Mistral museum, avenue Lamartine, Maillane* ☎ *90.95.74.06*
Tradition *Donkey cart fair, 1 May; music festival, Jul-Sep; Provençal festival, 15 Aug; La Temporada, bull-running or arena sports, Easter-1 Nov; Transhumance festival, Whit Mon.*
Walking *Van Gogh guided tours, Tues, Thurs and Sat from the Tourist Office.*

LES-SAINTES-MARIES-DE-LA-MER
Map ref 134 E2
Pop 2,000
Arles 38 km
Nîmes 57 km
Marseille 126 km
Toulon 194 km
Paris 796 km
🛈 5 avenue Van Gogh
☎ 90.97.82.55

An ancient and picturesque fishing port steeped in the tradition and folklore of the Camargue area, it is named after Mary Salome (mother of the Apostles James and John), Mary Magdelene and Mary Jacobe (sister of the virgin Mary) who are believed to have reached Provence with their

GYPSIES, LES STES-MARIES DE-LA-MER

THE CAMARGUE CATTLE AND HORSES

The Camargue is very largely aquatic, made up of pools and marshland, but its insubstantial land areas nonetheless provide support for two types of animal which live here in great numbers: the horses and cattle which are raised in ranches known in the Camargue as 'manades'.

The Camargue horses are descended from the 'equus caballus' portrayed by pre-historic artists in caves at Lascaux and elsewhere. Their strong, broad hooves enable them to move about safely on shifting soil without being shod. The horses are white, with heavy bodies and heads. As Frédéric Mistral wrote:

> For this wild breed
> Finds its true element in the sea
> Since, doubtless fleeing Neptune's chariot,
> They still bear flecks of foam.

Contrary to popular supposition, the 'rosse', the nickname for Camargue horses, is not left to run wild. It lives semi-free in the great expanses of the delta, owned by a 'manadier' or breeder and managed by the 'gardians'. Trained in past times to crush the grain, the horses are used nowadays more prosaically for visitors' trekking expeditions.

The Camargue bulls are as black as its horses are white. The result of continuous cross-breeding, it is small and has lyre-shaped horns. Domesticated in Roman times, they are not used, as in Spain, for bull fighting but for the courses à la cocarde. The local bullfights use Spanish bulls which are also bred in the Camargue.

This sport, open to all to watch and even take part in, can be seen in Arles, Tarascon, Beaucaire and Nîmes; after the abrivado when the bulls are brought into the town by the 'gardians', they are released into the arena or marked-off part of the town, with a 'cocarde' or plume between the horns which the 'razeteurs' try to pick off with a 'razet', a four-branched hook. Though the horns are usually trimmed, the spectacle is not without its piquancy.

RIBBON DANCE, LES STES-MARIES-DE-LA-MER

Ethiopian servant Sarah - patroness of gypsies. There are three pilgrimages each year; on a Sunday in October and the famous gypsy celebrations on 24 and 25 May, which attract considerable crowds. This is a colourful occasion when a procession of gypsies follow a statue of Sarah covered with jewels. Accompanied by girls in Arlésienne costume and 'gardians' from the Camargue who ride their horses into the sea, there is much feasting and revelry including Farandole dancing, sports with Camargue bulls and boat trips up the River Rhône.

The 12th to 15th century church is strongly fortified, to withstand the assaults of pirates and other barbarians. The flat

Hotels
Auberge Cavalière ****
route d'Arles
☎ 90.97.88.88
(and restaurant)
Le Mas de la Fouque ****
route d'Aigues-Mortes
☎ 90.97.81.02
(and restaurant)
Le Pont des Bannes ****
route d'Arles
☎ 90.97.81.09
(and restaurant)
Le Boumain ***
route d'Arles
☎ 90.97.81.15
(and restaurant)
Le Clamador ***
route de l'Amarée
☎ 90.97.84.26
L'Etrier Camarguais ***
chemin Bas-des-Launes
☎ 90.97.81.14
(and restaurant)
Le Galoubet ***
route de Cacherel
☎ 90.97.82.17
Hostellerie du Mas de Calabrun ***
route de Cacharel
☎ 90.97.83.23
(and restaurant)

Camping
Le Clos du Rhône ****
☎ 90.97.85.99
480 places Apr- Sep
La Brise ***
☎ 90.97.84.67
2,000 places open all year

Camargue region, natural habitat for a variety of birds, particularly flamingos, is also home to bulls and white horses around whom many of the local festivities revolve. The area can best be explored on horseback or, for the purposes of photography, aboard four-wheel drive vehicles.

Leisure
Beach 19 km of fine sand (plus naturist area).
Riding Numerous outlets offer accompanied treks into the area. Enquire at the Tourist Office.
Tradition Festo Vierginenco, third or fourth Sun in Jul; Grand Féria, 15 Aug; and gypsy pilgrimages 24-25 May, Sun nearest 22 Oct.
Watersports For equipment and boat hire, see Tourist Office.

SALON-DE-PROVENCE
Map ref 136 C1
Pop 35,000
Aix-en-Provence 35 km
Marseille 49 km
Nîmes 74 km
Toulon 114 km
Paris 764 km
ℹ 56 cours Gimon
☎ 90.56.27.60

Salon is at the heart of France's olive-growing region, set in lovely countryside heavy with the perfume of pine, thyme and lavender, with walks and rides along signposted footpaths.
A traditional market town which since 1936 has been the site of the French Air Force Officers' training college, the town itself has ancient squares and fountains shaded by tall plane trees. It was here that the astrologer Nostradamus wrote his prophecies.
The massive Château de l'Emperi which dominates the small town has a fine collection of military history from Louis XIV to the present day; the château's name refers to the medieval period when Salon-de-Provence belonged to the Holy Roman empire. The town also retained part of the ancient ramparts, many stylish old houses - including that of Nostradamus - and the fine churches of St-Michel and St-Laurent.
Salon is a good base for exploring the Etang de Berre and the Alpilles hills.

Leisure
Tradition Jazz festival, Jul.

Restaurants
Brûleur de Loups
avenue Gilbert le Roy
☎ 90.97.83.31
Impérial
1 place des Impériaux
☎ 90.97.81.84
Hostellerie du Pont de Gau
RN570
☎ 90.97.81.53

Hotels
Abbaye de St-Croix ****
route de Val-de-Cuech
☎ 90.56.24.55
(and restaurant)
Grand Hôtel d'Angleterre **
98 cours Carnot
☎ 90.56.01.10
(and restaurant)
Midi
518 allées de Craponne
☎ 90.53.34.67
Select Hôtel
35 rue Suffren
☎ 90.56.07.17

Camping
Nostradamus ***
route d'Eyguières
☎ 90.56.08.36
83 places Mar-Nov

Restaurants
Robin
1 boulevard G.-Clemenceau
☎ 90.56.06.53
La Brocherie des Cordeliers
20 rue d'Hozier
☎ 90.56.53.42
Le Café des Arts
20 place Crousillat
☎ 90..56.00.07

LAVENDER FIELDS, VAUCLUSE

SISTERON
Map ref 132 C2
Pop 7,000
Gap 47 km
Marseille 142 km
Toulon 204 km
Nîmes 216 km
Paris 714 km
🏛 Hôtel de Ville
☎ 92.61.12.03

A picturesque old town lying between Provence and Dauphiné, where an ancient citadel stands watch from a dramatic and deeply carved rock overlooking the neck of the Durance river and facing another rocky mass grooved by erosion. The houses of the old town huddle together along winding alleys and round the square, and admirers of Provençal Romanesque churches will appreciate the 12th-century former cathedral of Notre-Dame-des-Pommiers, as well as the tall clock tower with its wrought-iron belfry.

This is a land of sunny villages perched on slopes of gentle or rugged woodland beauty. The cool, fresh summer evenings are part of the exceptional qualities of this area, and it is a centre for a variety of outdoor sports and exploration.

Hotels
Grand Hôtel du Cours ***
allée de Verdun
☎ *92.61.04.51*
Les Chênes **
route de Gap
☎ *92.61.15.08*
(and restaurant)
Le Tivoli **
place du Tivoli
☎ *92.61.15.16*
(and restaurant)
De la Citadelle **
rue Saunerie
☎ *92.61.13.52*
(and restaurant)

Camping
Camping des Prés Hauts ***
☎ *92.61.19.69*
200 places May-Nov
Camping à la Ferme
Ferme de Saint-Domnin
☎ *92.61.06.84*

Restaurant
Les Becs Fins
16 rue Saunerie
☎ *92.61.12.04*

THE BAUME ROCK, SISTERON

Leisure
Aerial Sports Modern equipment and first-class gliding instruction is available from the Union Aérienne Sisteron Durance, Aérodrome de Vaumeilh, 04200 Sisteron ☎ *92.61.27.45. Piloting tuition for beginners will enable you to fly through the dramatic mountain scenery.*
Riding Centre Equestre Cante l'Abri, Vilhosc ☎ *92.61.38.15; Relais Equestre La Fenière at Peipin (6 km)* ☎ *92.64.14.02 and Club Equestre at Ribiers (8 km)* ☎ *92.65.14.60.*

PROVENCE'S BELL-TOWERS
The *campanile* is the name given in Provence to a bell-tower with a 'see-through' top. The bells hang in a wrought-iron structure instead of in the stone pinnacle of the more usual tower, which would not withstand the violent Mistral winds.

The photographer Etienne Sved has recorded 190 such towers and has classified them according to style; there are 'campanulé' bell-towers (the name 'campanile' refers to its borrowed campanula-flower shape), there are pyramids and spheroids, cosmological and bulbous designs. They can be found everywhere in Provence, from Sisteron to Aix-en-Provence and throughout the Haut-Var and the Lubéron. The beauty of these works of art is seen at its best in the little villages such as Puyloubier in the Aix region, at Lurs between Sisteron and Gap, Le Val in the Haut-Var, or at Crillon near Mont Ventoux.

Rock climbing Enquire at the Tourist
Office.
Tradition Music and drama festival,
second half of Jul.
Watersports Club de Canoe-Kayak de
Sisteron, 24 avenue du Jabron
☎ 92.61.34.18

TARASCON
Map ref 135 B4
Pop 11,000
Arles 18 km
Nîmes 26 km
Marseille 105 km
Toulon 173 km
Paris 744 km
🛈 59 rue des Halles
☎ 90.91.03.52

Facing its twin town of Beaucaire across
the broad River Rhône, Tarascon lay on
the frontier of the kingdom of Provence in
the days of King René. Threatening and
severe on the outside though with a
comfortable interior, this is one of France's
finest fortresses and stands on the site of a
Roman camp. In the 19th century Tarascon
was the setting for Daudet's boastful but
ineffectual comic hero Tartarin.
Now an agricultural centre, Tarascon
retains its old streets and Renaissance
houses, and the 19th-century Abbey of St-
Michel-de-Frogolet has pretty Romanesque
cloisters. The town has a splendid festival
at the end of June, parading its mythical

Hotels
Les Mazets des Roches ***
route de Fontvieille
☎ 90.91.34.89
(and restaurant)
De Provence ***
7 boulevard Victor Hugo
☎ 90.91.06.43
Les Echevins **
26 boulevard Itam
☎ 90.91.01.70
(and restaurant)
Le Provençal **
12 cours Artistide Briand
☎ 90.91.11.41
(and restaurant)

THE TARASQUE FESTIVAL, TARASCON

dragon, the Tarasque, and celebrating its
defeat with dancing, fireworks and general
festivities.
Across the beautiful suspension bridge,
Beaucaire also has a fine castle and
attractive old houses, and the Montagnette
hills nearby provide fine views over the
Rhône plain.
Leisure
Cycling Hire from Cycles Christophe, 70
boulevard Itam ☎ 90.91.25.85
Golf See Les Baux-de-Provence.
Riding Accompanied trekking, Mas de
Longalène, Grand Domaine de Frigolet
☎ 90.95.77.07
Tradition Festival and parade of the
Tarasque, four days around the last Sun in
Jun.
Walking Maps and suggested routes free
from the Tourist Office.

Camping
St-Gabriel
Mas Ginoux
☎ 90.91.19.83
50 places Mar-Oct
Le Tartarin **
route de Vallabrègues
☎ 90.91.01.46
80 places Mar-Sep

Restaurants
La Clé des Champs
quartier Saint-Gabriel
☎ 90.91.19.94
Lang Anh
2 avenue de la République
☎ 90.91.35.43

TOULON
Map ref 142 E2
Pop 181,000
Marseille 67 km
Nîmes 186 km
Paris 879 km
🗌 8 avenue Colbert
☎ 94.22.08.22

Toulon is a large modern city with a long history, set in a magnificent curving arc of tree-topped mountains behind its famous natural harbour. It was not exploited by either the Greek or Roman Empires - except that it was one of the most important sites for murex, a mollusc which could be boiled to produce very strong purple dye for the clothes of aristocratic Roman families. Apart from this industry, Toulon remained relatively unimportant until Provence was joined to France in the late 15th century. By Richelieu's time, however, Toulon was the centre of French naval construction in the face of threats from other Mediterranean fleets. Colbert, Louis XIV's minister, expanded the arsenal; marshes were drained, rivers diverted and fortifications extended.

The English occupied the city in 1793, supporting French Royalists, but Napoleon Bonaparte was appointed to attack them and the future Emperor gained one of his earliest victories here. In the 20th century, the city suffered considerable damage during the second World War.

Still a major naval centre, Toulon has its Naval Museum, place Monsenergues, with models of famous ships and battles as well as the Musée du Vieux-Toulon which illustrates local history. Ships were often manned by galley slaves who became a 17th-century tourist attraction. Today they can be seen depicted on the impressive portal of the old Hôtel de Ville. Monuments worth seeing include the cathedral in the heart of the medieval town, a mixture of Romanesque and 17th-century styles surmounted by a Louis XV wrought-iron belfry. The heart of the medieval town is undergoing pedestrianization and restoration of the old houses. There is a fine 18th-century fountain, Les Trois Dauphines, in the place Puget, and the market in the place Louis Blanc is one of the most famous in all Provence. The port, always an essential feature of Toulon, is busy and lively. Drive up to Mont Faron above the town for the best view of town and harbour; there is also a funicular railway which reaches nearly to the top, and a small zoo, making this an excellent expedition and one likely to appeal particularly to children.

Leisure
Boat Trips *Tours of the harbour operate throughout the season.*
Golf *Long, narrow private 18-hole course at Golf de Valcros, Domaine de Valcros, 83250 La Londe-les-Maures* ☎ *94.66.81.02*
Museum *Musée Naval, Ancien Fort de la tour Royale, Beaumont-Montfaron* ☎ *94.93.41.01 national memorial to the 1944 Provençal landings.*
Tradition *Music festival, opera, Jun-Aug; ancient music, May-Jul in town churches. Dance festival, Châteauvallon, Jul.*

Hotels
La Corniche ***
1 littoral F. Mistral
☎ *94.41.35.12*
(and restaurant)
Altéa la Tour Blanche ***
boulevard Amiral Vence
☎ *94.24.41.57*
(and restaurant)
Le Grand Hôtel ***
4 place de la Liberté
☎ *94.22.59.50*
L'Amirauté
4 rue Adolphe Guiol
☎ *94.22.19.67*
Continental Métropole **
1 rue Racine
☎ *94.22.36.26*

Restaurants
La Ferme
6 place L.-Blanc
☎ *94.41.43.74*
Le Dauphin
21 bis rue J.-Jaurès
☎ *94.93.12.07*

VAISON-LA-ROMAINE
Map ref 130 C2
Pop 5,000
Avignon 41 km
Nîmes 88 km
Marseille 135 km
Toulon 200 km
Paris 696 km
🛈 place du
Chanoine Sautel
☎ 90.36.02.11.

OLD VILLAGE, VAISON

The richness of Vaison-la-Romaine's past only became apparent in the early years of the 20th century, when its medieval and Roman remains were excavated. This pretty little town has fascinating Roman finds of the 2nd century BC city of 'Vasio', including street excavations complete with flagstones, baths and mosaics, and some beautiful marble statues, jewellery and pottery now gathered in the museum. The town itself is on the banks of the Ouvèze and its houses climb in tiers up to the "Haute Ville" at the foot of the old castle. The roman theatre is set in the hillside, facing the magnificent backdrop of Mont Ventoux. Vaison is popular now as a summer resort, and although the medieval castle in unsafe and closed, it is worth climbing up to it for the fine view of the surrounding plain and the hills beyond. The splendid Romanesque cathedral of Notre-Dame-de-Nazareth, based on an even older Roman structure, has some interesting Roman elements incorporated into it, and a beautiful early-Christian marble altar.

The large weekly market reveals Vaison's importance as a busy agricultural centre. This is a renowned area for the local black truffle as well as the Picodon cheese and lavender-scented honey. Looking beyond the town, rocky paths lead into the hills and there are numerous delights for walkers and painters, with magnificent panoramas of the wooded hills, the vineyards on the plain below and the mountains to the north.

Leisure
Riding Trekking at Centre de Loisirs Equestres, Le Prayal du Moulin, Entrechaux ☎ 90.46.03.24
Tradition Choralies, international choral festival, every third year, early Aug; music and drama festival in the Roman theatre, 10 Jul-10 Aug; Provençal festival, first Sun after 15 Aug.
Walking Ramblers' Association (FFRP) centre, Rasteau, Vaison-la-Romaine.
Wine Visit the cellars at Cave des Vignerons, Rasteau ☎ 90.46.10.43.

Hotels
Le Beffroi ***
rue de l'Evêché
☎ 90.36.04.71
(and restaurant)
Hôtel le Burrhus **
2 place Montfort
☎ 90.36.00.11
Le Logis du Château **
Les Hauts de Vaison
☎ 90.36.09.98
(and restaurant)
Les Aurics **
quartier des Aurics
route d'Avignon
☎ 90.36.03.15

Camping
Le Moulin de César ***
avenue César Geoffray
☎ 90.36.00.78
260 places Apr-Oct

Restaurants
Le Bateleur
place Th.-Aubanel
☎ 90.36.28.04
L'Amourié
avenue du Verdun
St-Romain-en-Viennois
☎ 90.46.43.72
La Table du Comtat
Seguret
☎ 90.46.91.49
Le Moulin à Huile
quai Maréchal Foch
☎ 90.36.20.67

PRACTICAL INFORMATION

TRAVEL INFORMATION

By Car

The international road sign system operates in France. Driving is on the right-hand side of the road and it is important to remember to yield right-of-way to the right when emerging from a stationary position. The French motorway system is run by private enterprise and tolls are levied on all the *autoroutes à péage*. Service stations with full facilities are located every 25km and there are also *aire de repos* or rest areas where motorists can break their journeys. In the event of a breakdown or accident on a motorway contact the police by using the emergency telephones sited every 2 km in orange posts. If the car electrics have failed, place the hazard warning triangle 45m behind your vehicle.

Speed limits

- open road 90 kmph = 55 mph approx
  dual carriageways 110 kmph = 68 mph approx
  towns and cities 60 kmph = 37 mph approx
  motorways 130 kmph = 80 mph approx
  Paris ring roads 80 kmph = 49 mph approx
- Seat belts must be worn, by law.
- Helmets must be worn on motorcycles and motorbikes.

The trafficjams at the beginning and end of August, when the whole of France seems on the move, are best avoided. During this period alternative itineraries or *itinéraires bis* (sometimes just *bis* for short) are signposted which take motorists away from the traditionally congested routes.
Up-to-date telephone information on road and traffic conditions in the region can be obtained from:
Circulation routière province
☎ 91.78.78.78
Inter service routes
☎ 48.99.33.33
3615 + autoroutes
3615 + iti (itinéraires)

Car Hire

If you are considering hiring a vehicle in France, car hire can be arranged locally by enquiring at the Tourist Office, or in advance by contacting any of the following international agencies. Because of the 33% tax levied, however, this will not prove a cheap exercise.
Avis
☎ 081-848 8733
Budget
☎ 0442 232555
Europcar
☎ 081-950 5050
Hertz
☎ 081-679 1799

By air

Principal airports serving Provence are Avignon, Nîmes/Arles and Marseille. All flights to France are handled by Air France, 158 New Bond Street, London W1Y 0AY
☎ 071-499 9511.

By sea

Cross-Channel ferries and hovercraft offer quick and cheap car and passenger crossings throughout the year. Brochures detailing crossings (some only operate during the summer months) and fares are available at travel agents nationwide. For details of ferry services to Corsica, Sardinia and North Africa contact:
SNCM
61 boulevard des Dames
Marseille
☎ 91.56.32.00

By train

The French railway system is run by the Société Nationale des Chemins de fer Française, or SCNF for short, and is the largest rail network in western Europe. Details of fares, routes and special deals and reductions are available from principal British Rail Travel Centres and continental rail-appointed travel agents. There are, for example, reduced rate tickets for families (*Rail Europ Family*), for senior citizens (*Rail Europ Senior*), for the under 26's (*Carré Jeune/Carte Jeune*) and for everyone there is the *France Vacances pass* and the *Billet Séjour*. Many stations offer a car hire service and over 240 of them also offer a cycle hire service.

GENERAL INFORMATION

Banks

Open regular hours Monday-Friday, 9am-12 noon and 2-4 pm, though most will be open all day in Paris or regional capitals. Some will open on Saturday mornings too if that is market day but stay closed on Mondays instead. Banks will not only close on, but also around, some public holidays - see National Holidays. This is known as *faire le pont,* literally 'bridging the gap'. In the case of banks, watch out for notices posted outside giving advance warning of such closures.

Emergencies and Problems

There are two emergency phone numbers:

Police and Ambulance **17**
Fire **18**

In the event of sickness, *pharmacies* or chemists' shops can provide addresses of local doctors and the nearest hospital casualty department. Some main hospitals, 'Centres Hospitaliers' (CH), teaching hospitals 'Centres Hospitaliers Universitaires' (CHU) and regional hospitals 'Centres Hospitaliers Régionaux' (CHR) are listed below:

Aix-en-Provence
CH, chemin des Tamaris
☎ 42.23.98.00
Arles
CH, J. Imbert
☎ 90.96.64.10
Avignon
SOS Medecin
☎ 90.82.65.00
CH, Henri Duffaut
☎ 90.80.33.33
Nîmes
CHR, CHU de Nîmes
☎ 66.27.41.11
Marseille
CH Allouche
☎ 91.68.90.33

Theft or loss

● Of car or personal belongings
Go to the nearest local or national police station, the *gendarmerie* or *Commissariat de Police.*
● Of passport or identity papers
Go to the local or national police station, consulate or embassy, or administrative police headquarters, the *préfecture.*
● Of credit cards
Go to the nearest local or national police station or to the *Mairie* or town hall and immediately notify:
Diner's Club ☎ (1) 47.62.75.00
Carte Bleue (Barclaycard and Visa)
☎ (1) 42.77.11.90
American Express ☎ (1) 47.08.31.21
Eurocard (Mastercard and Access)
☎ (1) 43.23.46.46
After reporting a theft or loss you will need a copy of the police's official report for a claim against your insurance on your return.

National Hoildays

Administrative offices and most shops close on public holidays. If any national holiday falls on a Tuesday or a Friday, the day between it and the nearest Sunday is also a holiday.

Le jour de l'an: New Year's Day, January 1
Lundi de Pâques: Easter Monday, date varies
Fête de travail: Labour Day, May 1
Ascension: Ascension Day, varies, according to Easter
Armistice '45: VE Day, May 8
Lundi de Pentecôte: Whit Monday, varies, according to Easter
Fête nationale: Bastille Day, July 14
Assomption: Assumption Day , August 15
Toussaint: All Saints' Day, November 1
Armistice'18: Remembrance Day, November 11
Noël: Christmas Day , December 25

THE MARKET IN APT

Shops

Food shops tend to open early, close at around midday for a lengthy lunch period and then re-open in the afternoon for another four hours or so. Many will open on Sunday mornings, staying closed on Mondays instead. In France, lunchtime is very definitely the time for lunch and not shopping or anything else. The police stations close, so do the museums and major sites, the lorries leave the roads and the streets empty as the restaurants and cafés fill. This is, incidentally, the perfect time to make distance on the roads which become miraculously clear during this period.

Market days

Aix-en-Provence: place d' Hôtel de Ville, flower market, every morning.
Arles: boulevard Emile Combes, Wednesday morning; boulevard des Lices, Saturday morning.
Avignon: les Halles and place Pie, Tuesday - Sunday near the porte St-Michel, open air market, Saturday.
Orange: place Clémenceau, open air market, Thursday.
Les Saintes-Maries-de-la-Mer: place des Gitanes, Monday and Friday.
Vaison-la-Romaine: town centre, Tuesday morning.

Weather

Short and medium-range forecasts
☎ 36.65.00.00 (by region)
Forecast for the Bouches-du-Rhône
☎ 36.65.02.13
Mountainous regions
☎ 36.65.04.04
Maritime forecasts
☎ 36.65.08.08

WHERE TO STAY

Out of season you can usually find accommodation en route and as the fancy takes you. The local Tourist Office which is known either as an *Office de Tourisme* or a *Syndicat d'Initiative*, can provide on-the-spot advice and information on accommodation availability. However, if your visit coincides with the peak holiday period, you shold make advance reservations for accommodation.

The *Comité Régional du Tourisme* as well as the Tourist Board for each of the *départements* within the region *(Comité Départemental du Tourisme)* will supply, on request, specific brochures detailing camping, hotel and self-catering *gîte* accommodation in their areas, from which you can make your choice.

General information on the region can be obtained by telephoning or writing to:

Comité Régional du Tourisme
22a rue Louis Maurel
13006 Marseille
☎ *91.37.91.22*

Specific information on the individual *départements* can be obtained by telephoning or writing to :

Alpes-de-Haute-Provence (04)
Comité Départemental du Tourisme
42 boulevard Victor Hugo
B.P. 170, 04005 Digne-les-Bains
☎ *92.31.57.29*

Bouches-du-Rhône (13)
Comité Départemental du Tourisme
6 rue du Jeune-Ancharsis
13001 Marseille
☎ *91.54.92.66*

Gard (30)
Comité Départemental du Tourisme
3 place des Arènes
B.P. 122, 30011 Nîmes
☎ *66.21.02.51*

Var (83)
Comité Départemental du Tourisme
B.P. 99, 83003 Draguignan
☎ *94.68.58.33*

Vaucluse (84)
Comité Départemental du Tourisme
2 rue St-Etienne
B.P. 147, 84008 Avignon
☎ *90.86.43.42*

CAMPING

There are probably more camp sites in France than any other country in Europe, and they enjoy an excellent reputation. Living under canvas can be wonderful fun as many of the sites are more like holiday camps in their provision of on-site shopping facilities and entertainment, and with such activities as riding, tennis, canoeing, etc, all laid on. Amenities do vary though and camp sites are officially star-graded as follows:

*	basic but adequate amenities
**	good all-round standard of amenities
***	first class standard with emphasis on comfort and privacy
****	very comfortable, low density and landscaped sites

All sites must display their grading and charges at the site entrance (for a family of four with tent, allow about 60FF for * site and 150FF for **** site per day). They must have roads connecting with the public highway and be laid out so as to respect the environment, with at least 10 per cent of the ground devoted to trees or shrubs. They must also have adequate fire and security precautions, permanent and covered washing and sanitary facilities, linked to public drainage, and daily refuse collection.

The maximum number of people per hectare, or about two and a half acres, is 300. However, at peak periods when all sites are under considerable strain, there may be some relaxation in the regulations. Sites graded ** and above must have communal buildings lit (and roads lit for *** and ****), games areas (with equipment for *** and **** sites), a central meeting place, points for electric razors, surrounding fence with a day guard (night watchman for *** and **** sites). Sites graded *** and **** must also have washing facilities in cubicles, hot showers, safe deposits, telephones and good shops on or close to the site.

GITES

These are Government-sponsored, self-catering rural properties which can be anything from a small cottage or village house, to a flat or part of a farm. Reasonably priced, they are ideal for families travelling by car and offer an economical way to meet and mix with the locals. The owner will be on hand to greet you when you arrive.

A small membership fee entitles you to a fully illustrated official handbook and free reservation service from the London booking office.

Contact Gîtes de France, 178 Piccadilly, London WIV 9DB
☎ 071-493 3480

More specific details for a particular location can be obtained by writing to the *Relais des Gîtes de France et de Tourisme Vert* for each *département*, the addresses for which are listed below:

Gîtes de France d'Alpes-de-Haute-Provence
rond-point du 11 novembre
04000 Digne-les-Bains

☎ *92.31.52.39 (guide costs 30FF)*
Gîtes de France de Bouches-du-Rhône
Domaine du Vergon
13370 Mallemort
☎ *90.59.18.05 (guide costs 25 FF)*
Gîtes de France de Gard
avenue Emmanuel d'Alzon
31020 Le Vigan
☎ *67.81.03.05 (guide costs 20FF)*
Gîtes de France de Var
rond-point du 4/12/74
B.P. 215, 83006 Draguignan
☎ *94.67.10.40 (guide costs 25FF)*
Gîtes de France de Vaucluse
Le Balance
B.P. 147, 84008 Avignon
☎ *90.85.45.00 (guide free)*

Chambres d'Hôte
Bed and breakfast accommodation in private homes, usually in rural locations. Local information on these available at the Tourist Offices.
Contact Gîtes de France Ltd
178 Piccadilly, London WIV 9DB
☎ 071-408 1343 and 071-493 3480
In France contact the addresses given above.

HOTELS
The French Government Tourist Office (FGTO), 178 Piccadilly, London W1V 0AL publishes a full list of hotel groups with details of booking offices in the UK as well as those French chains with whom you can book direct. They can also offer further advice and personal callers have a choice of three video terminals from which to select hotels of all categories.The official government star rating of hotels (Homologation Officielle du Ministère Chargé du Tourisme) is determined by the quality of accommodation, amenities and service on offer.

There are five grades , from * to ****Luxury and the prices quoted below are the minimum and maximum one might expect to pay per room.

****L	Luxury Hotel (palace) 520FF upwards	
****	Top class hotel 315-475FF	
***	Very comfortable hotel 210-365FF	
**	Good average hotel 125-260FF	
*	Simple but fairly comfortable hotel 95-140FF	

Prices are quoted per room whether occupied by one or two persons, though a few may offer a reduction for single occupancy.
Just as at camp sites, hotel prices must be displayed outside and inside the establishment. Most hotels with their own restaurant expect you to take dinner when staying the night. Full board or *pension* terms, i.e. room and all meals, is offered for a stay of three days or longer; half board or *demi-pension* terms for room, breakfast

and one meal are available outside the peak holiday period, and many hotels offer this in season too. Breakfast is not mandatory and you should not be billed for it if you haven't had it! Breakfast will be charged as a supplement varying between 15 and 77FF. When reserving accommodation, make sure the amount of *arrhes* or deposit is clearly stated, and ask for a receipt for any sum paid. When making telephone reservations, ensure that you state your arrival time, as hotels may re-allocate rooms after 7pm. If you find yourself delayed en route, make a courtesy phone call to the establishment stating your revised arrival time.
A selection showing the variety of hotel accommodation on offer follows. Where possible, the British representative of a French hotel chain is given.

Campanile
Small, modern ** hotels. Guide provides good street location maps.
Contact Campanile, Unit 8, Red Lion Road, Hounslow TW3 1JF
☎ 081-569 5757
In France Campanile, 31 avenue Jean Moulin, Marne-la-Vallée 77200 Torcy
☎ 66.62.46.46

Châteaux, Demeures et Tables des Vignobles
Converted château and other historic buildings offering top-class accommodation, their guide also includes a section on restaurants in wine-growing regions. See feature on page 119.
Contact FGTO, 178 Piccadilly W1V 0AL
In France Châteaux, Demeures et Tables des Vignobles, BP 40, F-13360 Roquevaire
☎ 42.04.41.97

Châteaux, Hôtels Indépendants et Hostelleries d'Atmosphère
Stylish private establishments, such as châteaux, hotels and castles, offering hotel-type accommodation and services but unaffiliated to any overseeing body. The illustrated guide book includes a section on restaurants. See feature on page 119.
Contact M. Farard, BP12, 41700 Cour Cheverny (no telephone)

Climat de France
Chain of 140 ** hotels throughout France.
Contact Voyages Vacances Ltd, 197 Knightsbridge, London SW7 1RB
☎ 071-581 5111
In France Climat de France, BP 93, 91943 Les Ulis
☎ (1) 64.46.01.23

France Accueil - Minotel Europe
Family-run ** and *** hotels, many with pools. Guide lists 160 across the country.
Contact France Accueil Hotels (UK) Ltd, 10 Salisbury Hollow, Edington, Westbury BA13 4PF ☎ 0380 830125

THE VAN GOGH GALLERY, ARLES

In France 85 rue de Dessous-des-Berges, 75013 Paris
☎ (1) 45.83.04.22

Grandes Etapes Françaises
Top-class accommodation.
Contact 140 rue de Belleville, 75020 Paris
☎ (1) 43.66.06.06

Ibis **
240 ** hotels throughout France.
Contact Resinter, c/o Novotel, Shortlands, Hammersmith, London W6 8DR
☎ 071-724 1000
In France Ibis **, 6-8 rue du Bois Briard, Courcouronnes, 91021 Evry
☎ (1) 60.77.27.27

Logis De France
Small and medium-sized family-run hotels with restaurant. Ideal for short breaks or motoring holidays, these hotels are mostly * and ** and are almost always rurally situated. They provide very good and reasonably priced accommodation.
Contact FGTO, 178 Piccadilly, London W1V 0AL for guide enclosing 80p in stamps.
In France Logis de France, 83 avenue de l'Italie, 75013 Paris
☎ (1) 45.84.70.00

Mapotel Best Western
160 *** and **** privately owned hotels throughout France.
Contact Best Western Hotels, Vine House, 143 London Road, Kingston-upon-Thames KT2 6NA
☎ 081-541 0033
In France 74 avenue du Dr Arnold-Netter, 75012 Paris
☎ (1)43.41.22.44

Mercure
A substantial chain with several hotels in Provence, primarily aimed at business travellers.
Contact FGTO, 178 Piccadilly, London W1V 0AL
In France Hôtel Mercure, 2 rue de la

Mare-Neuve, 91021 Evry
☎ (1) 60.87.43.20

Relais du Silence
This chain of 139 hotels specializes in offering locations of total peace and tranquillity for restful stays. A multi-lingual brochure is produced as the chain operates in many European countries.
Contact Hôtels Relais du Silence, 2 passage du Guesclin, 75015 Paris
☎ (1) 45.66.77.77

Relais et Châteaux
Luxury hotel accommodation and restaurant guide, with several locations in Provence featured.
Contact FGTO, 178 Piccadilly, London W1V 0AL for guide enclosing 80p in stamps.
In France Relais et Châteaux, 9 avenue Marceau, 75116 Paris
☎ (1) 47.23.41.42

Resthôtel Primevère
A chain of restaurant hotels at convenient stop-over points throughout France.
Contact FGTO, 178 Piccadilly, London W1V 0AL
In France Resthôtel Primevère, BP 66, 91223 Brétigny-sur-Orge
☎ (1) 64.49.74.74

YOUTH HOSTELS
This type of accommodation has always provided the young with a cheap and cheerful means of visiting another country. An International Youth Hostels membership card must first be obtained from:
The Youth Hostels Association (YHA) , Trevelyan House, St Albans, Herts
☎ 0727 55215
Other useful addresses:
Fédération Unie des Auberges de Jeunesse (FUAJ), 27 rue Pajol, 75018 Paris
☎ (1) 42.41.509.00
Ligue Française pour les Auberges de Jeunesse (LFAG) 38 boulevard Raspail, 75007 Paris
☎ (1) 45.48.69.84

BIENVENUE AU CHATEAU

The hotels, châteaux and homes presented here have been selected for several reasons: comfort, the quality of service, the beauty of their surroundings and their history. Each with a unique character, their charm will delight you.

The first six establishments belong to the chain known as **Châteaux, Demeures et Tables des Vignobles** and their brochure is available from BP 40, F-13360 Roquevaire ☎ 42.04.41.97 Bookings must be made direct with the proprietor.

Castel Lumière

Le Portail, 83330 Le Castellet Village (Var)
☎ 94.32.62.20
Contact M. Bernard Laffargue
Closed annually from 2 Nov-2 Dec
6 rooms (250-350FF)
From Castellet village there is a magnificent view over the vineyards and Lecques bay. Castel Lumière is renowned for its cuisine accompanied by the famous Bandol wines.

La Mas d'Aigret

Route D27A, 13520 Les Baux-de-Provence (Bouches-du-Rhône)
☎ 90.54.33.54
Contact M. Patrick Philip
Closed annually from 4 Jan-20 Feb.
14 rooms, 3 apartments (670-700FF)
This ancient farmhouse has a view from its terrace and swimming pool over miles of Provence countryside, as far as the Camargue. Swimming pool, table tennis, horse riding (2km), fishing (9km), and two golf courses (3mins and 10 mins).

Auberge Bourelly

13480 Aix-Callas (Bouches-du-Rhône)
Hameau de Callas, 7 mins from Aix-en-Provence
☎ 42.69.13.13
Contact M. et Mme Pons
Open all year
12 rooms, one suite (380-460FF)
A country farmhouse in the shade of century-old plane trees, this inn has several terraces and a large park. For relaxation there is a swimming pool, solarium, table tennis, French billiards and three golf courses nearby.

Hostellerie du Vallon de Valrugues

chemin de Canto Cigalo, 13210 St-Rémy-de-Provence (Bouches-du-Rhône)
☎ 90.92.04.40
Closed every Feb
48 rooms (600-820FF)
This is a fine Roman-style villa with a marvellous view over the Alpilles, the Lubéron and Mont Ventoux. Leisure activities include a swimming pool, tennis, sauna, spa, horse riding, table tennis, a putting green and a gym.

Mas des Capelans

RN 100, 84580 Oppède (Vaucluse)
☎ 90.76.99.04

MAS D'AIGRET, BAUX DE PROVENCE

AUBERGE DE CASSAGNE

Contact M. J.-P. Poiri
Closed annually from 15 Nov-15 Dec and
from 15 Jan-15 Feb
9 rooms (290-350FF)
This ancient Provençal farm is at the heart
of the Lubéron nature park between
Gordes and Oppède-le-Vieux. There is a
swimming pool and a park.

Les Agassins (auberge de Cassagne)
Le Pigeonnier, route d'Avignon
84130 Avignon - Le Pontet (Vaucluse)
☎ 90.32.42.91
Motorway exit: Avignon nord
Contact M. et Mme Mariani
Closed annually from 1 Jan-1 Mar
25 air-conditioned rooms (380-850FF)
In a century-old park 5 mins from the Palais
des Papes this inn has contemporary
architecture and the charm of a Latin
house. Facilities include a pool house,
horse riding, golf (7km), tennis (500m).

The following seven establishments have
been selected from the chain **Châteaux,
Hôtels Indépendants et Hostelleries
d'Atmosphère**. Their brochure can be
obtained from M. Farard, BP 12, 41700
Cour Cheverny.

Hotel Villa Borghèse
avenue des Thermes, 04800 Gréoux-les-
Bains (Alpes-de-Haute-Provence)

☎ 92.78.09.55
Contact M. J.-C. Redolfi
Closed annually fron 1 Dec-1 Mar
70 rooms (250-520FF)
Situated in Haute-Provence, this hotel has
a health and beauty centre with dietary
regimes and fitness programmes. For
leisure activities there is a swimming pool,
tennis coaching, horse riding (5km), golf
(20km), a bridge club with tournaments
and instruction. There are also opportuni-
ties for fishing.

Domaine de la Cride
13610 Le Puy Sainte-Reparade (Bouches-
du-Rhône)
☎ 42.61.96.96.
Contact M. et Mme Chosalland
Open all year but check first in winter
8 rooms (from 350FF)
On the slopes of Aix-en-Provence towards
the Lubéron, this beautiful country
farmhouse has a park of 2 hectares with a
little river running through it. Among the
recreational facilities are tennis (1km), a
swimming pool, horse riding, golf (10km)
and fishing.

Château de Vergières
13310 Saint-Martin-de-Crau (Bouches-du-
Rhône)
☎ 90.47.17.16
Contact M. et Mme Jacques Barbier

MAS DE LA BRUNE

Closed annually from 15 Nov-1 Mar
6 rooms (570-660FF)
In the peaceful surroundings of a 350
hectare estate in the midst of meadows
and in the shade of trees which are
centuries old, the château offers high
quality of comfort. For your relaxation there
is tennis (8km), a swimming pool (8km),
horse riding (8km), golf (15km).

Mas de la Brune
13810 Eygalières (Bouches-du-Rhône)
☎ 90.95.90.77
Closed annually from 1 Nov to Palm Sunday
9 rooms and 1 suite
Children over 12 years are welcome. In a
delightful setting this consular house
exudes charm. The vaulted press room is
used as a dining room and there are rooms
with old style, fabric-hung walls and a
heated Roman swimming pool. Horse
riding (2km), golf (15km).

Hostellerie le Roy Soleil
route des Baumettes, 84560 Menerbes
(Vaucluse)
☎ 90.72.25.61
Contact M. Derine
Closed annually from 15 Nov-15 Mar
14 rooms (380-720FF)
Near Gordes, this genuine 17th-century
home is hidden amid vines and cherry
trees and with the fortified village close by

and the wild Lubéron countryside all
around. Tennis and swimming pool are
available with horse riding (3km), golf
(12km) and fishing (14km)

Domaine le Moulin Blanc
chemin du Moulin, Les Baumettes, 84220
Gordes (Vaucluse)
☎ 90.72.25.41
Contact S. Herail, P. Robert
Open all year
18 rooms (500-980FF)
In the past this inn was a staging post, then
a flour mill and today is very well
appointed. It has a huge chimney, a
canopied bed and a park of 3 hectares.
Swimming pool, tennis, golf, and horse
riding nearby.

Hostellerie du Prieuré
rue J.-B. Aumard, 84480 Bonnieux
(Vaucluse)
☎ 90.75.80.78
Contact Mme Charlotte Keller and M. Rémi
Chapotin
Closed annually from 5 Nov-15 Feb
10 rooms (310-440FF)
This 18th-century town house is situated at
the foot of the village ramparts. Meals are
served in the garden or in front of the fire
according to the season. Tennis (100m),
swimming pool (10km), horse riding
(10km), golf (20km).

ATLAS

Easy to handle and full of useful information, you will find
this 18-page atlas of IGN mapping an invaluable
travel companion.

It begins with a double-page general map of the region
(scale 1:1,200,000) enabling you to identify all the towns
and major places of interest as well as estimate the
distances between them. Page references to the more
detailed maps of the area (scale 1:250,000) are shown on
the grid of this general map.

The legend on page 125 lists all the symbols used on the
maps, particularly those denoting places of interest to the
tourist: churches and châteaux, historical buildings and
curiosities, panoramic views and natural features. A colour
code is used on the maps to differentiate between sites
judged to be "an absolute must", "interesting" and
"worth seeing".

Beside each town listed in the gazetteer, you will find the
corresponding map reference. The gazetteer section also
includes street plans of the main towns.

Used in conjunction with the rest of the guide book, this
accurate, easy-to-read map section is your key to the
region of France you are about to explore.

LEFT THE PAVILION OF QUEEN JEANNE, BAUX-DE-PROVENCE
ABOVE HORSES IN THE CAMARGUE

IGN MAPS

As the French saying goes: "He who travels far cares for his horse...", to which one could equally add .." and takes with him his IGN maps"! Essential to your travels in France, IGN maps through their extensive and definitive range, meet every conceivable requirement.

FRANCE IN 16 MAPS
The Red Series
These maps are perfect for driving tours when getting to know a region. Their scale is 1 : 250,000 (1cm = 2.5km).

FRANCE IN 74 MAPS
The Green Series
Ideal for sporting use such as horse-riding, mountain-biking, canoeing etc. Their scale is 1 : 100,000 (1 cm = 1 km)

FRANCE IN 2,000 MAPS
The Blue Series
These highly-detailed topographical maps are popular for walking, climbing and countryside exploration off the beaten track.

Their scale is 1 : 25,000 (1cm = 250m). From these have been developed a new practical series called the 'TOP 25' : top for topographical and 25 short for the scale size 25,000. The particular qualities of these maps are their re-designed large format covering one specific tourist area (one 'TOP 25' map replacing four or five conventional Blue Series maps). They carry a large amount of tourist and practical information enabling visitors to pinpoint with great accuracy the natural and other landmarks of the area. There are at present 90 titles with another 300 planned for the near future.

FRANCE FROM THE AIR
With their unique view of towns, holiday areas and sites of particular interest, the beautifully coloured IGN aero-posters and aerial photographs provide a detailed perspective of the French landscape.

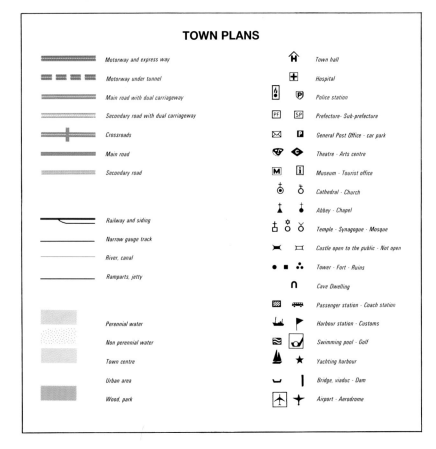

TOWN PLANS

Motorway and express way	Town hall
Motorway under tunnel	Hospital
Main road with dual carriageway	Police station
Secondary road with dual carriageway	Prefecture - Sub-prefecture
Crossroads	General Post Office · car park
Main road	Theatre - Arts centre
Secondary road	Museum · Tourist office
	Cathedral · Church
	Abbey · Chapel
Railway and siding	Temple · Synagogue · Mosque
Narrow gauge track	Castle open to the public - Not open
River, canal	Tower · Fort · Ruins
Ramparts, jetty	Cave Dwelling
	Passenger station - Coach station
Perennial water	Harbour station - Customs
Non perennial water	Swimming pool · Golf
Town centre	Yachting harbour
Urban area	Bridge, viaduc - Dam
Wood, park	Airport - Aerodrome

LEGEND

	1	2
Motorway (1) - motorway standard (2)		

	1	2	3
Main road with separate roadways (1), Main roads (2) (3)			

Secondary roads

Other roads : regularly maintained (1), not regularly maintained (2), Footpath (3)   1   2   3

Distances in kilometres (between ⌀ or two outlined cities)   2,5   3,5
6

Railways : double track (1), single track (2) - Station or stopping place (3),   1   2   3   4
open to passenger traffic (4)

Boundary of region (1), of departement (2), of State (3)   1   2 PF   3

Navigable canal (1), non navigable canal (2) - Salt pans (3) - Marsh or swamp (4)   1   3   4
2

Area exposed at low tide : Beach (1) - Rocks (2)

Wood

Airports : international (1), with hard runway (2), without hard runway (3).   1   2   3

TOURISM

Cathedral - Abbey - Church - Chapel

Castle - Castle open to public - Prominent building

View point - Curiosity

District of interest to tourists - Spa - Winter sports resort

Civil architecture (ancient house, bastide, covered market) - Rampart

Ancient remains - Interesting ruins - Memorial

Pilgrimage - Traditional festival - Museum

Military cemetery - Cave - Shelter - Lighthouse

Tourist railway - Rack railway - Aerial cableway, cable car or chair lift

Custom-houses : French, foreign

ITINERARIES

Drive

Walk

Cycling tour

Canal-river cruise

PLACES OF INTEREST

Not to be missed

Interesting

to see

Scale 1: 250 000

Kilomètres 5   3   1   0   5   10   15 Kilomètres

INSTITUT GÉOGRAPHIQUE NATIONAL

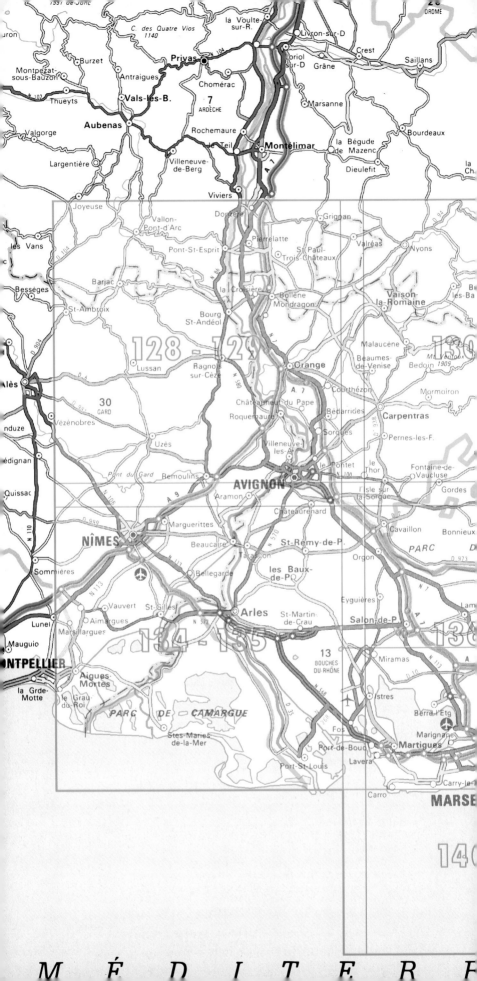

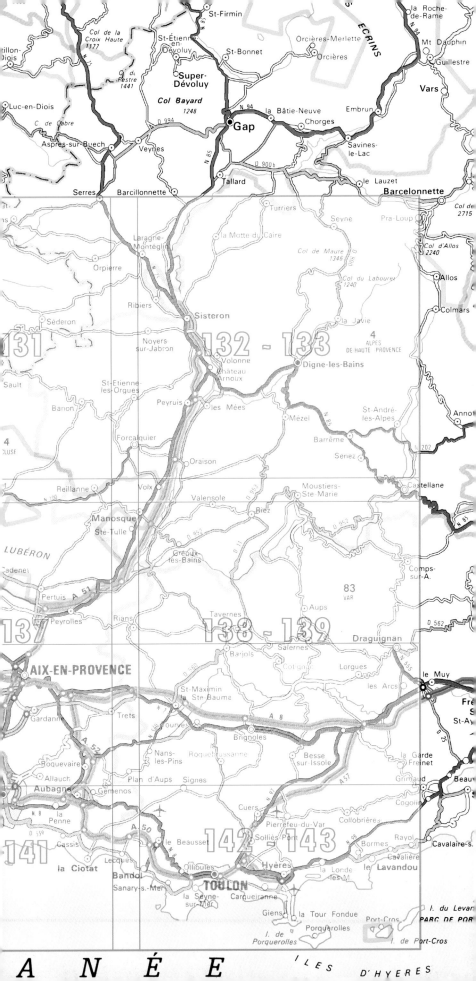

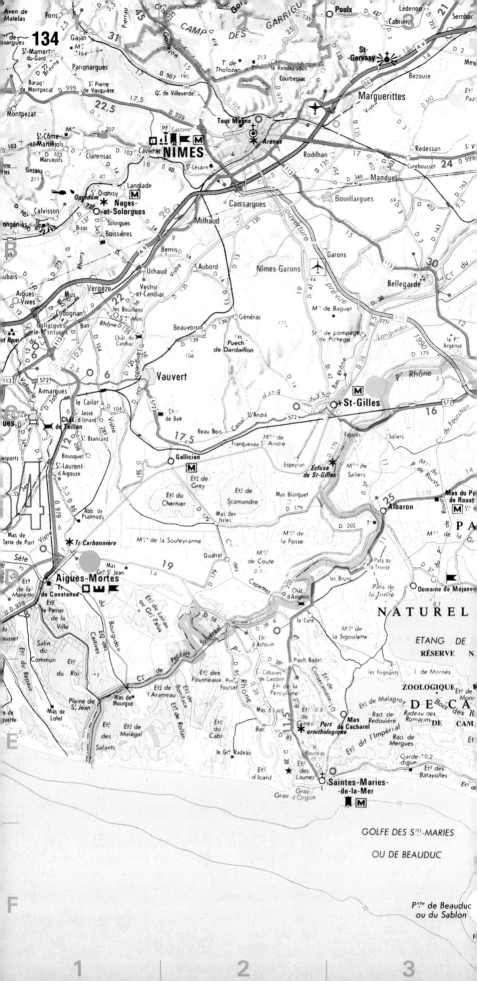

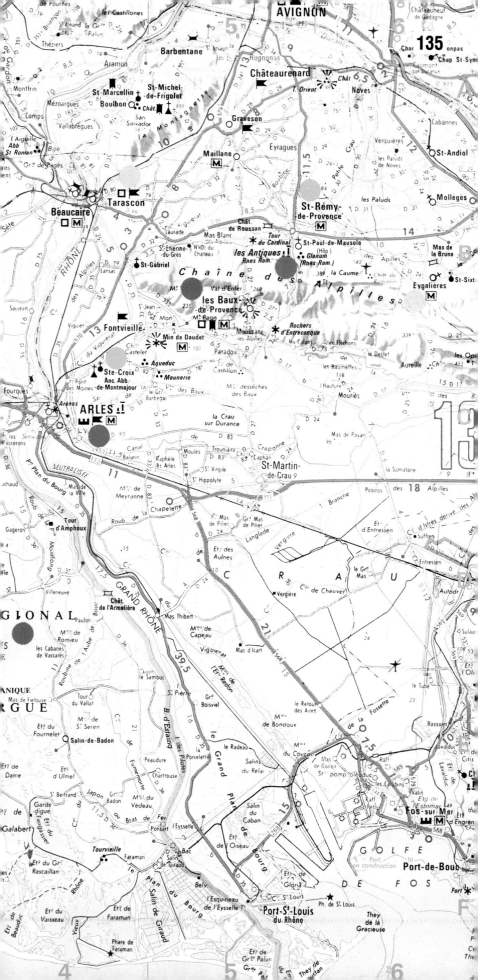

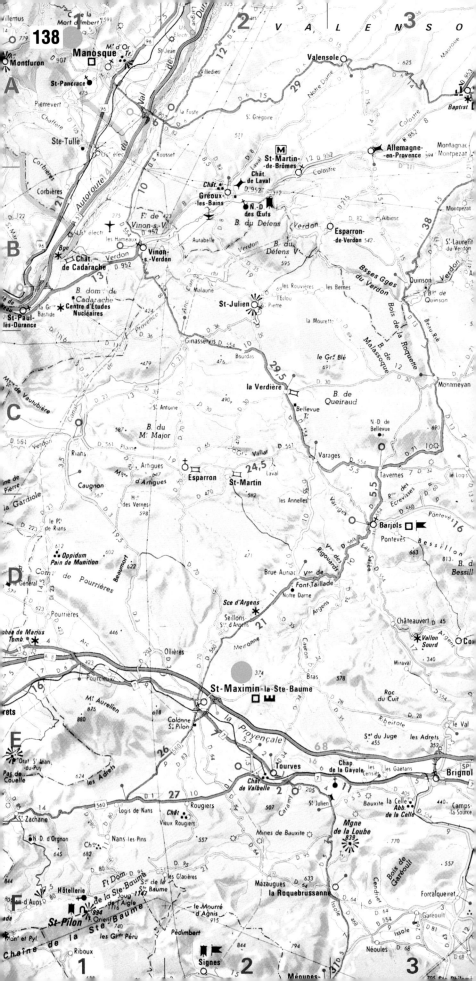

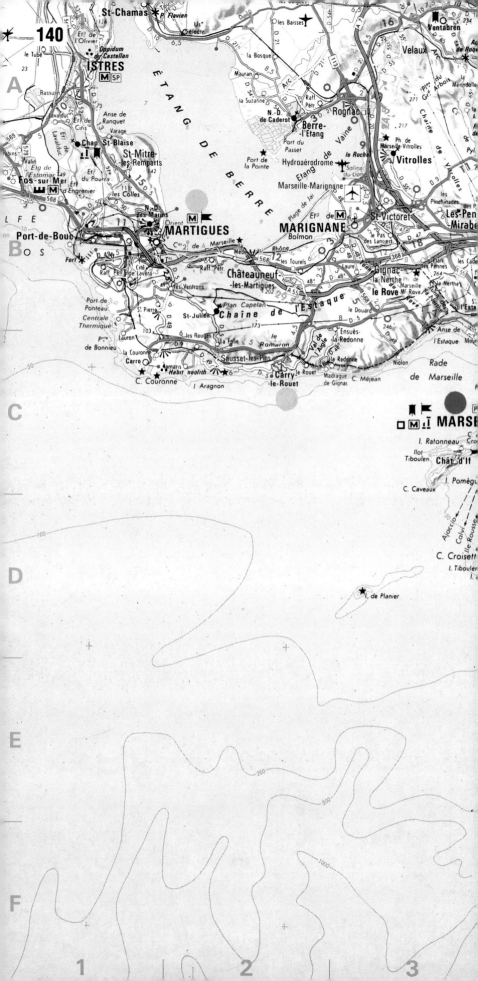